BS
680
.E9
S86

Stock
The way in the wilderness.

North Dakota
State Library Commission
Reference Library
Bismarck, N. D.

RULES

BORROWERS — Residents of North Dakota without adequate local public library service are entitled to draw books from this library by signing an application blank which will be furnished on request.

NUMBER OF VOLUMES — Any reasonable number of books may be borrowed at one time for the purpose of study.

TIME KEPT — State borrowers may keep books four weeks. Books may be renewed for original loan period.

POSTAGE—Return postage must be paid by the borrower.

OVER-DUE BOOKS—A fine will be charged for books kept overtime.

The
WAY IN THE WILDERNESS

The

WAY IN THE WILDERNESS

Exodus, Wilderness and Moses Themes in
Old Testament and New

by
Augustine Stock, O.S.B.
Abbey of the Immaculate Conception

THE LITURGICAL PRESS
Collegeville, Minnesota

Nihil obstat: John Eidenschink, O.S.B., J.C.D., *Censor deputatus. Imprimatur:* ✠ George H. Speltz, D.D., Bishop of St. Cloud. October 16, 1968.

Typography, layout and printing by the North Central Publishing Company, St. Paul, Minn.

Contents

Introduction

The Bible contains many different kinds of writings, written over a period of more than a thousand years, yet it displays an amazing unity. And it could not be otherwise, since the Bible contains "the human witness to One who was pursuing a single, self-consistent plan and was getting, in some measure at least, the response that he desired."[1]

The Old and the New Testament are inseparably bound together by a pattern of promise and fulfillment. Standing alone the Old Testament is only half of an arch. It finds its counterpart in the New Testament and only in the New Testament. Numerous events and themes appearing in the Old Testament reappear in the New by way of continuity or contrast. The Bible shows us the one saving Lord at work in Old Testament and New and it is inevitable that his saving acts should bear a strong family likeness. There is a real, objective likeness uniting the saving events of the Old Testament and the New. Then, in various ingenious ways and for various purposes, the inspired writers of the New Testament use these patterns, by way of continuity or contrast, to set forth the fact of salvation through faith in Jesus.

Christians needed the Old Testament in order to explain Jesus. What meaning could Christians "attach to the unique event which had turned their lives inside out?"[2] The only way to interpret the Christian fact was through the Old Testament. With love, Christians tied themselves to this history in order to understand their own experience. "The New Testament writers made use of the rich and profound theology of the Old Testament, and of the forms in which it was cast, in order to portray, in the very way their story was told, not only that certain events took place, but that in taking place they possessed a specific theological sig-

---

[1] N. W. Porteus, "Theology of the Old Testament," in *Peake's Commentary on the Bible*, 152.
[2] J. Guillet, *Themes of the Bible*, 13.

vii

nificance to which the Old Testament forms and stories were, in their view, a divinely appointed anticipatory type."[3]

HISTORY-CENTEREDNESS

One of the strongest links joining the Old Testament and the New is their common history-centeredness. This is a unique feature of biblical faith. It makes certain assertions because certain things have happened. In the Bible "we do not deal with timeless truths that are related only incidentally to historical circumstances, but with truth that is inseparably related to specific times, places, and peoples."[4] Biblical faith is based on the conviction that God acts and reveals himself in history.

Not, of course, that all history is revelation. When God acts to reveal himself in history he also supplies an accredited interpreter. "We have first the announcement of the significant fact of history through a prophetic person, speaking in the name of God, then the fulfilment of the announcement, and finally the interpretation of the event by one whose credentials were supplied by the fulfilment."[5] Moses said he would lead the Israelites out of Egypt, a deliverance he was powerless to effect. The deliverance came, not by the Israelites' own efforts, but by the help of wind and wave, which Moses could not control.

Revelation through history and revelation through persons, the personal and the impersonal factors, are intimately linked and offer a check on each other. Full acceptance of the biblical assertion remains an act of faith but the act of faith is intellectually respectable. Revelation through history is no mere deduction on the part of a clever and gifted people from what has happened. It is no unprovable assumption or projection of human faith into history. The deed is revelation and the meaning of the deed is revelation, which is appropriated by faith.

THE DECISIVE EVENT

Among all those historical events in which God is seen to act and reveal himself, one is primary and fundamental from every

[3] J. Marsh, "Theology of the New Testament," in *Peake's Commentary on the Bible*, 756.

[4] B. Anderson, *Understanding the Old Testament*, vii.

[5] H. H. Rowley, *Unity of the Bible*, 66.

point of view — the Exodus from Egypt. In the preface to the Decalogue the Lord declares: "I am the Lord your God who brought you out of the land of Egypt, out of the house of bondage" (Exod. 20:2). This divine act of deliverance is the core of Old Testament revelation, the starting point of all biblical revelation. The Exodus was the decisive historical experience that formed the Hebrews into something they had not been before — a self-conscious historical community, a people, the People of God. It led the people Israel to recognize God's right to impose upon them the covenantal relationship with all that it involved. The Exodus therefore represents the starting point of that plan of salvation which finds its realization in Jesus of Nazareth. And as the first decisive saving act, the Exodus established the pattern, as it were, for all future divine saving acts.

It was the Exodus that set the Israelites to writing as well. A unique event, one of its products is a unique collection of writings, the Old Testament, and, indeed, the New Testament also. In the process of writing the Exodus was so decisive that earlier happenings and subsequent experiences were seen in its light. It was from within their covenant faith that the Israelites turned their attention to their earlier history. They recalled and recorded the history of their ancestors, the great patriarchs, in the light of this faith. Ultimately the Exodus revelation became the point from which the doctrine of God as creator of heaven and earth was affirmed. But above all, the Exodus revelation cast its light over the future, since it made manifest the Lord's intention to carry out a plan of salvation. And ultimately the Exodus event became "the basis also for the confident hope that beyond any fulfilment of itself in any historical occasion, it would be the clue to the meaning and the recognition of what God would finally do with his world."[6]

Two Kerygmas

Since the one Lord is carrying out the one plan of salvation in the Old Testament and the New, it is inevitable that a family likeness should be discernible throughout, that like patterns of events and themes should appear on the Old Testament level

[6] J. Marsh, *op. cit.*, 756.

only to appear again on the New Testament level, by way of continuity or contrast. Thus, both the Old Testament and the New begin with a kerygma: a proclamation of the saving acts of God. After the deliverance from Egypt, the Lord led the Hebrews to Sinai and proclaimed to them: "You have seen what I did to the Egyptians, and how I bore you on eagles' wings and brought you to myself. Now therefore, if you will obey my voice and keep my covenant, you shall be my own possession among all peoples; for all the earth is mine, and you shall be to me a kingdom of priests and a holy nation" (Exod. 19:4-6). The Hebrews had experienced the Lord's saving activity in the events of the Exodus and on that basis they are summoned to faith, to the covenant bond.

The New Testament revelation also begins with a kerygma. After Jesus of Nazareth's resurrection from the dead and the coming of the Spirit, St. Peter proclaims the realization of the Lord's definitive act of deliverance in Jesus' death and resurrection, and he invites all men to share in this deliverance by having faith in Jesus: "There is salvation in no one else, for there is no other name under heaven given among men by which we must be saved" (Acts 4:12). And when it came to writing, the new, definitive Exodus played a role analogous to that of the first Exodus. As earlier happenings and subsequent experience were seen in the light of that first Exodus, so it was from within a realized salvation that the Church turned her attention backward to Jesus' public life, his infancy, and ultimately to his pre-existence. And it was from within this realized salvation that the Church looked to the future and the full actualization of the salvation already won.

Both Testaments flow from a kerygma and the two kerygmas are intimately connected. In the Old Testament the primary emphasis is "that the God in whom Israel believes is a God who acts and reveals himself in history. The New Testament *kerygma* or proclamation of the acts of God in Christ is both reinforced by what we may call the Old Testament *kerygma* and supplies us with a criterion by which to measure it, as well as with an experience which predisposes us to accept it."[7]

Christians needed the Old Testament to explain Jesus; they

[7] N. Porteus, *op. cit.*, 152.

needed the Exodus to explain the New Exodus. Using the rich and profound theology of the Old Testament, and the forms in which it was cast, the New Testament writers could not only indicate effectively that certain events had taken place but could at the same time bring out the religious meaning of these events. "At the fountain source of Israel's life was an event, and that event was the redemption from Egyptian bondage. It gave Israel new words, a new way of speaking, and a history. The Exodus is for Israel what the death and resurrection of the Christ are for the new Israel, and the new Israel could do no other than employ the imagery and words of the redemption from bondage when it proclaimed redemption from a deeper and more terrible slavery."[8]

The Exodus was the decisive event, the great watershed, in Israel's history. "Even today the Jewish people understand their vocation and destiny in the light of this revealing event which made them a people and became their undying memory. Just as the Christian remembers and relives the sacrifice of Jesus Christ in the celebration of the Lord's Supper, so the Jew recalls and makes contemporary the Exodus as he celebrates the Passover."[9] In both Old Testament and New we have one central event, or rather complex of events, which assimilates other historical traditions to itself, generating both a new doctrine of creation and a new anticipation of the "end of the world." The New Exodus, however, is not merely placed alongside or offered instead of the Exodus story, but, on the contrary, is deliberately related to it as both fulfilling and transcending it.

In the prologue to his popular *Introducing New Testament Theology*, A. M. Hunter writes: "The Bible is the book of the People of God; or, if dynamic terms are preferred, the Book of the two Exoduses."[10] The Old Testament recounts the story of the first Exodus: the Lord's election of his people, his rescuing them from Egyptian bondage, and the covenant he made with them at Sinai, whereby they became the People of God. In the succeeding centuries the Lord led and guided his people by the prophets he sent them, blessed and punished them according to

8 J. Muilenburg, *The Way of Israel*, 49.
9 B. Anderson, *op. cit.*, 5.
10 P. 9.

their faithfulness to the covenant, and kindled in their hearts the hope of a Day when his saving will would be fully realized.

The New Testament is the story of the fulfillment of the divine plan of redemption. God sent his Son, Jesus of Nazareth, to inaugurate the Kingdom of God by his passion and death. "This is the Second Exodus (cf. Luke 9:31), and this is the event we call 'the Fact of Christ.' By this phrase we mean the totality of what Jesus Christ's coming involved, his person, work and words, of course, but also the Resurrection, the advent of the Spirit and the creation of the new Israel destined to become the Catholic Church."[11]

The Exodus theme is, therefore, one of the most basic in biblical tradition and it is to be expected that it should appear again and again as the Lord's plan of salvation unfolded. It is possible to trace out this theme as it is reflected in the various writings of Scripture and such an exercise should add greatly to our understanding of the Lord's saving purpose. And with the Exodus theology as a background, we may profitably consider two closely related themes. After the Exodus from Egypt there followed the wilderness period, the march through the desert, which also left a deep imprint on biblical tradition. So after the Exodus there follows a consideration of the Wilderness theme. God's chosen agent throughout this period was Moses, who consequently came to occupy a unique place in biblical tradition. The Moses theme will be our third area of study.

[11] *Ibid.*

The
WAY IN THE WILDERNESS

Part One

THE EXODUS
OLD TESTAMENT

THE EXODUS FROM EGYPT

After the Hebrews had been living in Egypt for many generations, "there arose a new king over Egypt, who did not know
Joseph" (Exod. 1:8). The former benevolence and protection
were changed to hostility and repression. The Hebrews were re-
duced to the status of state slaves and were put to work building
the store cities of Pithom and Rameses in the Delta region of
the Nile.

And it came to pass that a young Hebrew was brought up and
trained at the Pharaoh's court. He was given the name Moses.
Despite his upbringing, however, he retained a strong feeling of
identification with his Hebrew kinsmen. One day when he was
grown he saw an Egyptian taskmaster beating a Hebrew slave
and slew him (Exod. 2:11-15). Fearing that the news of this
secret murder would reach the king's ear, Moses fled into the
land of Midian, in northern Arabia, east of the Sinai peninsula.
There he married the daughter of Jethro (Reuel), the priest of
Midian (Exod. 2:15-22).

While tending his father-in-law's flock, Moses came to Mount
Sinai and there the Lord spoke to him. The Lord told Moses that
he had seen the affliction of the Hebrews who were in Egypt:
"I know their sufferings, and I have come down to deliver them
out of the hand of the Egyptians, and to bring them up out of
that land to a good and broad land. . . . Come, I will send you
to Pharaoh that you may bring forth my people, the sons of Israel,
out of Egypt" (Exod. 3:8, 10).

1

The fact that Moses was a Hebrew and felt an identification with his kinsmen might offer some explanation of his returning to Egypt, but it offers no explanation of his doing so in the name of a God called Yahweh. "Moses said to God, 'If I come to the people of Israel and say to them, "The God of your fathers has sent me to you," they will ask me, "What is his name?"'" (Exod. 3:13). The people in Egypt would not recognize Yahweh as the name of their God. "God said to Moses, 'I am the Lord. I appeared to Abraham, to Isaac and to Jacob, as God Almighty, but by my name the Lord I did not make myself known to them" (Exod. 6:2-3). All this is borne out by the fact that after their deliverance, the Israelites made a covenant with this God, which would have been unnecessary if Yahweh was already their God.

After receiving his revelation and commission in Midian, Moses goes to the Pharaoh and demands that the Hebrews be allowed to go out into the desert to sacrifice to Yahweh. When the Pharaoh refuses, the Lord sends the plagues upon the land of Egypt. At length the Pharaoh said, "Go forth from among my people and go serve the Lord, as you have said" (12:31). So Moses and the Hebrews left in haste. The Exodus narrative expresses the conviction that the Lord was guiding them on the way, taking an active part in the course of events. We read that "the Lord went before them by day in a pillar of cloud to lead them along the way, and by night in a pillar of fire to give them light" (13:21, J). They are a "mixed multitude" (12:38), representing not only descendants of Jacob but also Habiru of other origins.

THE SEA DRIVEN BACK

Leaving the land of Goshen the group came to a marshy area, a shallow extension of the Gulf of Suez. In the meantime, however, the mind of the Pharaoh changed and he set out with army and chariot in pursuit of the fugitive slaves and overtook them encamped at the sea. Then "the Lord drove the sea back by a strong east wind all night" (Exod. 14:21), so that the fugitives were able to cross during the night. But "when the horses of Pharaoh with his chariots and his horsemen went into the sea, the Lord brought back the waters of the sea upon them. . . .

Then Miriam, the prophetess, the sister of Aaron, took a timbrel in her hand; and all the women went out after her with timbrels and dancing. And Miriam sang to them:

> Sing to the Lord, for he has triumphed gloriously;
> the horse and his rider he has thrown into the sea."
>
> (Exod. 15:19-21)

This is one of the oldest pieces of poetry in the Old Testament, and in all probability it originated during the very event it celebrates.

It is not at all likely that the Israelites invented this story of their deliverance from Egyptian slavery. If they had invented the story, they would have ascribed their deliverance to the God they had hitherto worshipped. And if Moses had taken the mission on himself, he would have presented himself to the enslaved Hebrews in the name of their God. Rather Moses goes to them and, in Yahweh's name, promises a deliverance neither he nor they can bring to pass. Their efforts play no part in the story. When the Pharaoh comes down upon the fugitives, Moses again promises a deliverance, but not by his hand or theirs. "Moses said to the people, 'Fear not, stand firm, and see the salvation of the Lord, which he will work for you today" (Exod. 14:13). The fugitives did not stand and fight. If they had done so, we may be sure that their traditions would have cherished the memory.

The crossing of the Red Sea occurred when an east wind drove the waters back. This need not be a wholly miraculous occurrence. Such a thing is not impossible in this marshy area, where the waters are shallow. In fact, it has been witnessed at other times. But, as H. H. Rowley writes in his *The Faith of Israel*: "To regard this timely help as a chance coincidence offers no explanation of the return of Moses to Egypt, or the confidence he had known that Yahweh would deliver the people. Neither could his confidence control the powers of Nature and bring about the timely help. Both sides of this story must be remembered. There was the prophetic personality of the man who appeared in the name of God to promise a deliverance he and the Israelites were helpless to effect; and there was the historic event of the deliverance which responded to his prior promise."[1]

[1] P. 42.

THE COVENANT

Then the fugitives turned their backs on Egypt and plunged into the trackless waste of the Sinai peninsula, Mount Sinai their destination. The journey was very difficult. Water was scarce; there was no food. It was a time of murmuring, discontent, and rebellion against Moses, and, above all, lack of faith. But the indomitable Moses kept the group going and at length they staggered into the oasis of Sinai.

The fugitives had come to the place where Moses himself had responded to Yahweh's initiative. Now the group as a whole was to experience what Moses had experienced earlier — a call to respond to the Lord's historical plan of salvation. Through Moses the Lord announces to the Hebrews: "You have seen what I did to the Egyptians, and how I bore you on eagles' wings and brought you to myself. Now therefore, if you will obey my voice and keep my covenant, you shall be my own possession among all the peoples; for all the earth is mine, and you shall be to me a kingdom of priests and a holy nation" (Exod. 19:4-6).

The Lord had manifested himself by saving acts, delivering them from Egyptian bondage ("You have seen what I did"). But this divine initiative demands a response. The group is placed in a situation of decision, summoning them to a task within the divine purpose.

After three days there is a divine appearance (theophany) on Mount Sinai and Yahweh utters the Ten Commandments. By his saving acts the Lord has demonstrated that he is a just, moral, and merciful God — that he hates injustice and rescues those in distress. From now on this "mixed multitude" of slaves he has rescued are to be *people* and his own chosen people, his instrument of salvation. Therefore they too must be moral and just. The Ten Commandments are the terms of the covenant Yahweh is making with his people, spelling out the core of their obligations.

All that remains now is to give the covenant a living reality by the blood ritual. The ceremony is described in Exodus 24. Moses built an altar at the base of Mount Sinai and set up twelve pillars, "according to the twelve tribes of Israel" (v. 4). Animals are sacrificed and half the blood is dashed against the altar, as a symbol of Yahweh's participation in the rite. The other half is put in basins, and Moses "took the book of the covenant, and read it in the hearing of the people; and they said, 'All that the Lord has spoken we will do, and we will be obedient.' And Moses took the blood and threw it upon the people, and said, 'Behold the blood of the covenant which the Lord has made with you in accordance with all these words'" (Exod. 24:7-8).

The Lord gave his people a covenant. Since he is the Lord of the universe, he cannot submit himself to obligations as men do. His covenant with the Israelites was not a parity covenant — one in which the parties bind themselves to obligations on an equal footing. The people of Moses' time also knew of another kind of covenant, the suzerainty covenant, such as a king would make with a vassal. To his vassal, the suzerain "gives" a covenant. And within the covenant the vassal finds protection and security, provided he observes the terms of the agreement. The most striking aspect in this type of covenant is the attention given to the sovereign's deeds of benevolence in favor of his vassal. The vassal's motive for obedience is that of gratitude for what has been done for him.

In the first eighteen chapters of the book of Exodus is related all that the Lord had done for the fleeing Hebrews. Then Moses is commissioned to announce to them the purpose for which Yahweh had brought them to Sinai: "You have seen what I did. . . . Now therefore, if you will obey my voice and keep my covenant, you shall be my own possession among all peoples" (Exod. 19:4-5).

THE CENTRAL EVENT

The Exodus event stands at the heart of biblical faith. It made a mixed multitude of Hebrews into the people Israel and gave them their distinctive faith. It was in the light of this faith that they were to write their earlier history, and this faith was to guide or to pass judgment on all their later actions. "A stream, we say, never rises higher than its source. This proverb may be applied to the source of Israel's faith in the Mosaic period. In subsequent periods the stream widened, its channel was deepened, its flow was interrupted by many cataracts. But Israel's greatest moments of worship and prophetic insight were regarded as a return to the source: the Exodus and the covenant of Sinai."[2]

[2] B. Anderson, *op. cit.*, 59.

It was from within their covenant faith that in the course of time the Israelites turned their attention to earlier history and made this, too, part of their traditions and scriptures. First they dealt with the patriarchal period, and concerning this period they possessed traditions closely related to what was going on in the Fertile Crescent at that time. "The Exodus or deliverance from Egypt is the central or focal point in Israelite history and faith. When Israel claimed to be the Chosen People, she was giving the only explanation possible to her for this historical event. Looking back at the tradition of the Fathers it was only natural that the doctrine of election should be traced to Abram, the Patriarchal father of the people (Gen. 12:1-3), as the sole explanation for his leaving home and kindred for a land of which he knew nothing. In all of our main historical sources the deliverance from Egypt is seen as the fulfilment of God's promises to the Patriarchs."[3]

Ultimately the Israelites came to deal with the primeval period, but in this case the legends they made use of are not anchored to anything with which the modern historian can deal. But as the historical assertion becomes fainter, the theological teaching becomes proportionately stronger and more imposing.

The line of composition, therefore, runs backward from the Exodus to creation, while the story line, of course, runs in the opposite direction. If we consider the Pentateuch from the latter point of view we see that from Adam to the Tower of Babel the human tragedy increased, despite advances in the arts and sciences. The Tower of Babel passage is the climactic evidence of that self-assertion which prompted men to revolt against their Creator. "Come, let us build ourselves a city, and a tower with its top in the heavens, and let us make a name for ourselves" (Gen. 11:4). But God intervened and confused their tongues. At the end of primeval history man finds himself shut out from life's fullness — life in communion with God and in community with his neighbor.

But then in Ur of the Chaldeans, God speaks to Abram and says: "Go from your country and your kindred and your father's house to the land that I will show you. And I will make your name great, so that you will be a blessing" (Gen. 12:1-2). Abram

---

[3] G. E. Wright, *The Old Testament Against Its Environment*, 49f.

is an individual but in the mind of the sacred writer, the Yahwist, writing from within his covenant faith, Abram and the other patriarchs are the personification of the people whom the Lord has called and covenanted. In any case, these patriarchs are wanderers toward a goal that Yahweh has set before them. Their history is a nomadic movement from promise toward fulfillment, not an aimless quest for pastureland for their flocks.

To anchor the great patriarch even more securely in Israel's tradition, the later Priestly Writer describes the Lord's making a covenant with Abram. At this time the patriarch's older name Abram (meaning, "may the [divine] Father be exalted") was changed to Abraham, a name the writer takes to mean "father of a multitude." In the context of the Semitic doctrine of names, this change, like others in the Scriptures, indicates the deep significance of Abraham's vocation.

CROSSING JORDAN

So decisive an event was the Exodus that earlier happenings and subsequent experiences were seen in its light. It was from within their covenant faith that the Israelites wrote an account of their earlier history. But above all, the Exodus revelation cast its light over the future, manifesting the Lord's intention to carry out a plan of salvation, ultimately becoming the clue to the meaning and the recognition of what God would finally do with the world. The New Israel employs the imagery and words of the first Israel's redemption from Egyptian bondage when it proclaimed redemption from a deeper and more terrible slavery. Israel's greatest moments of worship and prophetic insight subsequent to the Exodus were regarded as a return to the source: the Exodus and covenant of Sinai.

Later generations used the Exodus motif both to interpret other past events and as a means of describing and foretelling the shape of future events. But in these uses of the Exodus, the significant thing, for us and even for the original writers, is not the physical affinities that the use of the imagery may assert but the theological fact of the act of God to deliver, and in some sense thus to constitute or reconstitute, his people.

After the covenant-making at Sinai, Israel spent forty years

wandering in the wilderness south of Beer-sheba. During this
time the people were forged into greater unity and solidarity
through bitter struggle and suffering. Too weak to break past the
fortresses guarding the southern approach to Canaan, Israel had
to take the long circuit through the country of Transjordan. Refused permission to travel on the King's Highway, Israel skirted
Edom and Moab. Approaching the Amorite kingdom of Sihon,
they again sent messengers asking permission to use the King's
Highway. The king not only refused but sent an army to crush
Israel (Num. 21:33-35). But the battle resulted in a great victory
for Israel and they took possession of a large strip of territory in
Transjordan. There they encamped, just across the Jordan near
Jericho, and the stage was set for an invasion of the Promised
Land.

After three days' encampment, Joshua said to the people:
"Sanctify yourselves; for tomorrow the Lord will do wonders
among you" (Jos. 3:5). In the crossing of the Red Sea, Moses
stretched out his hand over the sea and the waters were divided, "and the people of Israel went into the midst of the sea
on dry ground, the waters being a wall to them on their right
hand and on their left" (Exod. 14:22). So in the crossing of the
Jordan, when the feet of the priests bearing the ark touched
the waters, "the waters coming down from above stood and rose
up in a heap . . . and Israel passed over on dry ground" (Jos.
3:16, 17). In the first instance "the Lord drove the sea back by
a strong east wind" (Exod. 14:21). This need not be an entirely
miraculous event, as we have seen. But that it should happen in
the nick of time, and in that particular sequence of events, af-
forded a reasonable ground for faith.

A similar set of circumstances appeared with the crossing of
the Jordan. In his commentary on the book of Joshua in *Peake's
Commentary*, H. G. May suggests that "perhaps as the Israelites
were preparing to cross, an earthquake caused the banks of the
Jordan to collapse. An Arab historian, Nuwairi, reports that in
December of the year 1267 a mound which overlooked the river
on the west fell into the Jordan and dammed it up so that the
water ceased to flow down for about 16 hours. A similar occurrence took place in 1909. More recently, in 1927, the high west
bank collapsed below the ford Jisr ed-Damîyeh, which is about

half a mile from Adam, and dammed the river, cutting off the water from the river-bed below it for 21½ hours."[4] Again, while this
may not be an entirely supernatural event, its happening at a
certain precise time and place, and in the given sequence of
events, and with qualified interpreters at hand, could mark this
as a historical event in which the Lord was revealing his saving
power. In this instance there would seem to be even physical
affinities between the original and the subsequent exodus. This
would have strengthened the place of the Exodus tradition in the
memory of the People of God and assured its further use.

EXODUS FROM BABYLON

Israel came in out of the desert, gradually took possession of
Canaan, and became agriculturalists. Then began a fierce struggle between faith and culture, between faith in Yahweh and the
ritual myths which pretended to assure the fertility of the land.
Frequently Israel fell away. Israel said: "I will go after my lovers,
who give me my bread and my water, my wool and my flax, my
oil and my drink" (Hosea 2:5). Then the Lord sent prophets to
recall the Israelites to their covenant obligations. The prophets
warn them that unless they return to the Lord they will have to
return to the desert. "They shall return to the land of Egypt, and
Assyria shall be their king, because they have refused to return
to me" (Hosea 11:5).

And this did indeed happen. The ten tribes in the north were
carried off by the Assyrians and did not return. Then the Babylonians destroyed Jerusalem and carried off most of the remaining
Jews. Once again the People of God found themselves subject to
a foreign power. If the Lord was to realize his saving purpose
through them a New Exodus was called for. This New Exodus
is proclaimed in Second Isaiah. In the first part of the book of
Isaiah (cc. 1–30), Israel is still living in Judah under the kings
of the house of David, Jerusalem is still regarded as the Lord's
city that he will not allow to fall, and the Temple is still standing.
But in the latter part of the book (Second Isaiah, cc. 40–66), a
radical change in the historical situation is apparent. Judah is
desolate, the Temple lies in ruin, and the people are in Baby-

---

4 P. 292.

lonian exile. The Assyrians, Israel's scourge in Isaiah's day, are
no longer a menace. Babylonia is mistress of the world and even
her rule seems to be nearing an end. Cyrus of Persia, the Lord's
"shepherd and messiah" (Is. 44:38; 45:1), will soon decree a return from exile and a rebuilding of Jerusalem and the Temple.

The Way in the Wilderness

While Isaiah of Jerusalem spoke the language of warning and
rebuke, Second Isaiah is "the book of consolation." A divine judgment has occurred, Israel has been punished. Now Second Isaiah
proclaims a New Exodus. He speaks of pardon, deliverance, and
restoration for a despairing people.

> Speak tenderly to Jerusalem,
>   and cry to her
> that her warfare is ended,
>   that her iniquity is pardoned,
> that she has received from the Lord's hand
>   double for all her sins (Is. 40:2).

With intense feeling the prophet speaks to the holy people in
exile, suggesting that her hard service is at an end.

> A voice cries:
> "In the wilderness prepare the way of the Lord,
>   make straight in the desert a highway for our God.
> Every valley shall be lifted up,
>   and every mountain and hill be made low;
> the uneven ground shall become level,
>   and the rough places a plain.
> And the glory of the Lord shall be revealed,
>   and all flesh shall see it together,
>   for the mouth of the Lord has spoken" (Is. 40:3-5).

These opening verses express Second Isaiah's central message,
which is an announcement of the imminence of salvation for
exiled Israel. The "voice" is either a poetical equivalent for "Thus
says the Lord," found so often in the prophets, or the voice of a
member of Yahweh's heavenly council evoked from the vision
during which Isaiah had received his prophetic office (chapter

6). The "voice" introduces the primary theme of a "highway for our God." The return from exile is in some sense a return of Yahweh himself, bringing his flock with him (v. 11), and involves a revelation of the Lord's glory, a concept that is also prominent in Isaiah's inaugural vision. "All flesh shall see [the glory] together" (v. 5); all mankind will be united in the day of fulfillment.

In subsequent passages this new deliverance is connected even more explicitly with the deliverance from Egypt. Thus in Isaiah 43 we read:

> Thus says the Lord,
>   who makes a way in the sea,
>   a path in the mighty waters,
> who brings forth chariot and horse,
>   army and warrior;
> they lie down, they cannot rise,
>   they are extinguished, quenched like a wick:
> "Remember not the former things,
>   nor consider the things of old.
> Behold, I am doing a new thing;
>   now it springs forth, do you not perceive it?
> I will make a way in the wilderness
>   and rivers in the desert.
> The wild beasts will honor me,
>   the jackals and the ostriches;
> for I give water in the wilderness,
>   rivers in the desert,
> to give drink to my chosen people,
>   the people whom I formed for myself
> that they might declare my praise" (Is. 43:16-21).

The God who will send to Babylon is the God who has already led his chosen people from bondage to freedom. The "way in the sea" refers to the passage of the Red Sea. As then a way was made through the water, so now through the desert mighty obstacles will be overcome. Plainly the Exodus is included with the "former things," and the "new thing" is the New Exodus, now unfolding before their eyes. Future remembrance will not be (as in the Passover) of the escape from Egypt, but of the new act of redemption. Water in the desert was one of the great gifts of the period of the wandering through the desert. So now God's provision will be bountiful.

Great as were the wonders of the Exodus, they will be surpassed by those which accompany this new deliverance. In the old, Yahweh made a way for his people by drying up the sea; in the new he will provide abundant water in the desert. When the sea was divided, the fish died for want of water (Is. 50:2), but in the New Exodus the animals of the desert will have an abundance of water.

Chapter 48 concludes with a direct command to the exiles to leave Babylon: "Go forth from Babylon, flee from Chaldea, declare this with a shout of joy, proclaim it." Exodus imagery is used to describe the divine protection the returning exiles will enjoy during this New Exodus. "They thirsted not when he led them through the deserts; he made water flow for them from the rock; he cleft the rock and the water gushed out" (Is. 48:20-21). The imagery of this verse is that of the Exodus and the language is verbally related to Psalm 105:41.

A NEW CREATION

Chapter 51 of Isaiah contains this striking passage:

> Awake, awake, put on strength,
>   O arm of the Lord;
> awake, as in days of old,
>   the generations of long ago.
> Was it not thou that didst cut Rahab in pieces,
>   that didst pierce the dragon?
> Was it not thou that didst dry up the sea,
>   the waters of the great deep;
> that didst make the depths of the sea a way
>   for the redeemed to pass over?
> And the ransomed of the Lord shall return,
>   and come to Zion with singing;
> everlasting joy shall be upon their heads;
>   they shall obtain joy and gladness,
>   and sorrow and sighing shall flee away (Is. 51:9-11).

Here the prophet represents Israel crying out to Yahweh in a daring address, imploring him to manifest his power over the forces of evil as he did in the creation and in the first Exodus. The Jews and others in the ancient world believed that the act of creation had involved God in a tremendous struggle against the supernatural forces of evil and chaos. Here the prophet uses ancient mythological language of the East which originally told of creation and is here descriptive of the Exodus. The thought is: Let the New Exodus begin. Rahab, the dragon, the sea and the great deep are all expressions of the original chaos. The word "deep" (*tehom*) is equivalent to Tiamat, the Babylonian name for the Chaos monster. Rahab is the Western Semitic name for the same mythical dragon. There is an allusion here, as in many other poetical passages of the Old Testament, to a popular myth current in Canaan corresponding to the Babylonian myth contained in the epic *Enuma elish.*

Let the Lord intervene on behalf of his people and manifest his power as he did at the creation of the universe and at the time of the Exodus. "Arm of the Lord" recalls the Lord's promise to the Hebrews in Egypt that he would bring them out from under the Egyptians "with an outstretched arm and with great acts of judgment" (Exod. 6:6). In mythological thought the power of Chaos was identified with the ocean, with its restless might, so fearsome to non-seafaring peoples. But God overcame and restrained the power of Chaos in creation, as is evidenced by his dividing the waters and setting limits to the sea. Therefore when the Lord divided the Sea of Reeds to allow the fleeing Hebrews to escape from Egyptian bondage, the Lord again asserted his power over the power of Chaos. He "cut Rahab in pieces, he pierced the dragon." Since the ocean, rivers, and springs are part of the great abyss on which the earth rests, the Lord's drying up the sea, the "waters of the great deep," represents a victory over Tiamat.

So now let the Lord's arm put on strength to work similar deeds for the exiles in Babylon, assuring a New Exodus. It is interesting to note that the *Magnificat* proclaims the definitive answer to this prayer. "He has shown strength with his arm, he has scattered the proud in the imagination of their hearts" (Luke 1:51).

The Lord answers the people's prayer by citing a prophecy already spoken by Isaiah (35:10). It should suffice for them that this prophecy has been made with Yahweh's authority; for no human power can prevent its fulfillment. "The ransomed of the Lord shall return, and come with singing to Zion; everlasting joy shall be upon their heads; they shall obtain joy and gladness, and sorrow and sighing shall flee away" (v. 11).

EXODUS REAPPLIED

As dictated by the Old Testament revelation as a whole, Second Isaiah looks upon the Exodus as the decisive event of Israel's past. It was the time of Israel's creation, even as it was the time of her redemption. In this event the Hebrews were made the people of God even as they were rescued. Looking to the future, Second Isaiah portrays Israel's imminent liberation from the bondage and despair of the Babylonian exile in imagery drawn from the Exodus tradition: the flight from Egypt, the deliverance at the Sea of Reeds, the march through the wilderness, the triumphant journey toward Canaan, the Promised Land.

"Moreover, he blends with this historical tradition imagery drawn from the old creation myth, according to which Creation was the outcome of a fierce conflict between the Dragon of Chaos (called Tiamat) and the Creator. As we have pointed out before, this myth (found in *Enuma elish*) figured prominently in Babylonian religion, and was transmitted to Israel through the Canaanites. But in Israel's faith the mythology is transformed by being blended with the remembrance of Yahweh's deeds *in history*. According to Second Isaiah's poetic imagination, the waters of the Red Sea, through which Israel crossed long ago, were the waters of Chaos, hostile to Yahweh's creative and redemptive act. And just as Yahweh's arm was victorious in that conflict, so in the present historical situation he comes as the victor on behalf of his fainting people. To the Deep he says, 'Be dry,' and through the midst of the waters he prepares a way for the people to pass over (44:27)."[5]

And so it came about that the imagery of the creation came to be applied to the Exodus. How proper then that Second Isaiah views the approaching redemption as a new beginning, a New Creation. In the new age God will make all things new. "In God's creative work there is no boundary between 'nature' and 'history,'

[5] B. Anderson, *op. cit.*, 410.

for both men's lives and the natural setting will be marvelously
transformed (41:17-20). The wilderness, which the prophet identifies with the waste places of Judah, will be converted into a
garden like Eden (51:3; cf. 41:17-20; 43:19-21). Above all, there
will be a New Israel, bound to Yahweh in a new relationship
(54:4-10), and with a 'new song' on her lips (43:10-12)."[6]

DELIVERANCE FROM SIN

One of the central motifs in Second Isaiah's message, therefore,
is that of the New Exodus. But Second Isaiah contains not only
an amplification of the themes of the Exodus. His book contains
a new and noteworthy element. Israel now finds herself in captivity. Unlike that of Egypt, the captivity is a punishment. Israel
had sinned against God, so God delivered her into the hands of
her enemies. Right at the head of Second Isaiah's book stands the
declaration that deliverance is now at hand for Israel, because
she has now satisfied for her sins. "Speak tenderly to Jerusalem,
and cry to her that her warfare is ended, that her iniquity is par-
doned, that she has received from the Lord's hand double for all
her sins" (Is. 40:2).

The political servitude that Israel had to undergo "is the consequence and sign of another servitude, more mysterious and far
more profound — the servitude of sin! That is why 'the Servant'
whom God raised up to deliver His people (Is. 42:1-9; 49:1-6;
50:4-11; 52:13–53:12) would take upon Himself the sins of the
Israelites in order to free them (Is. 53:5-12). The new Exodus
could be performed only through the blood of the Servant that
was shed in expiation for the sins of men."[7]

THE PSALMS

A concept as basic as the Exodus was certain to be celebrated
in the Psalms and there the theme received its most vivid and
colorful expression. Thus Psalm 114 reads:

When Israel went forth from Egypt,
     the house of Jacob from a people of strange language,

---

[6] *Ibid.*, 411.
[7] J. Giblet et al., *The God of Israel, the God of Christians,* 222.

Judah became his sanctuary,
  Israel his dominion.

The sea looked and fled,
  Jordan turned back.
The mountains skipped like rams,
  the hills like lambs.

What ails you, O sea, that you flee?
  O Jordan, that you turn back?
O mountains, that you skip like rams?
  O hills, like lambs?

Tremble, O earth, at the presence of the Lord,
  at the presence of the God of Jacob,
who turns the rock into a pool of water,
  the flint into a spring of water.

This is a good example of how the Exodus absorbs earlier happenings and subsequent experiences. Creation, Exodus, entrance into Canaan, and, possibly, the New Exodus are brought together. The hymn celebrates the wonders of the Exodus and the entry into Canaan, yet the poetical language may have been influenced by the theme of the quelling of the forces of nature in the myth of creation. And like many of the Psalms which deal with the Exodus, "there is an implied comparison with the second Exodus, the return from the exile and Babylon."[8]

In the first instance, "the mountains skipping like rams" is a reference to the earthquake at Sinai, "but there is probably a blend here of Israel's national traditions with the myth of God's triumph at creation over the unruly forces of chaos."[9] The Lord's turning "the rock into a pool of water" reminds us of a number of passages in Second Isaiah (41:18-20; 43:16-21) where there is a comparison between the old Exodus and the new. The earth is admonished to tremble. "Not the sea and the mountains, as at the Exodus, but the earth alone, because the new Exodus is from Babylon."[10]

We find the same combination of ideas expressed in an even

[8] E. Kissane, *Book of Psalms*, II, 204.
[9] G. W. Anderson, "The Psalms" in *Peake's Commentary*, 438.
[10] Kissane, *op. cit.*, 205.

more picturesque way in Psalm 74. This wonderful psalm seems
to have been written after the destruction of Jerusalem by the
Babylonians. Zion lies in ruins, the Temple has been plundered,
the festivals are at an end, the people are without prophet or
teacher. But the psalmist affirms his faith that the Lord who acted
to save and to create in the past will act to deliver and re-create
in the future.

> Yet God my King is from of old,
>   working salvation in the midst of the earth.
> Thou didst divide the sea by thy might;
>   thou didst break the heads of the dragons
>   on the waters.
> Thou didst crush the heads of Leviathan,
>   thou didst give him as food
>   for the creatures of the wilderness (Ps. 74:12-15).

Again, much of the imagery may be paralleled in Babylonian
and Ugaritic mythology. The seven-headed monster Lotan (Leviathan) is mentioned in Ugaritic texts as in conflict with Baal.
But it is Israel's historical situation that the psalmist has in mind.

It would seem that the psalmist wishes to evoke the ideas of
both the conquest of the powers of Chaos, which was the prelude
to the work of creation, and the wonders of the Exodus, described figuratively as a renewal of this conquest of Chaos. On
the one hand, the Hebrew poets do allude frequently to a popular version of the myth current in Canaan, while, on the other
hand, Rahab and the Dragon are sometimes used as figures for
Egypt. The Lord manifested his power in creation and the imagery of the popular myth is used in the poetic evocation of this
event. And since there is a parallel between the Lord's subduing
Chaos and dividing the waters in creation, and his dividing the
waters and slaying the Egyptians in the Exodus, the imagery finds
a new application. The imagery would seem to evoke both events,
of necessity.

In creation the Lord divided the waters of the abyss, which at
times is personified as Rahab, leader of the forces of Chaos. The
Lord "divided the sea and broke the heads of the dragons." In
the Exodus the Lord divided the sea, subduing the forces oppos-
ing his will and delivering his people. The Lord "crushed the

heads of Leviathan and gave him as food for the creatures of the wilderness." After the people of Israel walked on dry ground through the sea, they "saw the Egyptians dead upon the seashore" (Exod. 14:30).

The conquest of Chaos was the prelude to the work of creation. The waters were separated from the land and by cleaving the dry land God created the springs and rivers, which have their source in the abyss beneath the earth. At the Exodus, the God who created the rivers dried them up to make a way for his people.

The Exodus motif, then, would seem to be one of the central themes of the Old Testament as a whole. The Old Testament was organized around it. Earlier happenings and subsequent experiences were seen in its light. "By the time that our earliest present literary references to the events of the Exodus were written down, that occasion had already become the focal point of the story of God's bringing his people into historical existence. But these earliest references are, as our present evidence suggests, separated by something like 300–500 years from the historical occasions they recount. The biblical story is ineradicably theological; it was meant to say not only that Israel escaped from Egypt, not only that God acted in a certain way on that night, but, even more, that what God did on that occasion can be properly understood only in the light of what had been done before, and of what was done afterwards, and was still to follow. The Exodus, that is to say, became part of the history of the people of God, and the *crux interpretationis* of that history."[11]

And since the Old and the New Testaments are two parts of one whole, the Exodus motif is certain to be an important one in the New Testament as well.

NEW TESTAMENT

The Old and the New Testaments are inseparably bound together by a pattern of promise and fulfillment. The first Christians needed the Old Testament in order to explain Jesus. The New Testament writers make use of the theology of the Old Tes-

[11] J. Marsh, *op. cit.*, 757.

tament, and the form in which it was cast, in order to portray, not only that certain events took place, but also to set forth their religious meaning. And since the Exodus experience was primary and fundamental in the Old Testament, the Exodus motif was bound to occupy an important place in the New.

So the Bible stands before us as the book of the two Exoduses. The Old Testament relates the story of the Lord's covenant with his people, Israel, and his rescuing them from Egyptian bondage in the first Exodus. In the succeeding centuries the Lord guided and disciplined his people through the prophets he sent them and through his judgments and mercies, gradually purifying and elevating their religious thinking and kindling in their hearts the hope of a Day when he would bring about a New Exodus, his definitive saving act. The New Testament, for its part, is the story of the fulfillment of the divine plan of salvation in the life, death, and resurrection of Jesus, and his continued presence among us during this interim age of the Church in mystery, looking forward to the full realization of this saving act with the consummation of all things.

ST. MARK
THE ESCHATOLOGICAL PROPHET

St. Mark's Gospel begins with the declaration that this is "the beginning of the gospel of Jesus Christ, the Son of God" (v. 9). This is the "good news" concerning a man, Jesus of Nazareth, who has fulfilled the Old Testament promise. He is the Anointed, the Christ, the Messiah; and more, he is the Son of God. The activity of Jesus' Precursor, John the Baptist, is itself the fulfillment of hopes and prophecies and it is the immediate sign that the Lord's saving will was to be realized. After covering Mark in his article on "The Theology of the New Testament," John Marsh writes: "How may we summarise, then, the basic theological themes of Mark? The Gospel tells the story of the beginning of a new Israel or Son of God in the divine human person of Jesus. It brings the story of the Exodus to provide categories of interpretation to the life and death of Christ."[12]

[12] *Op. cit.*, 762.

John's coming had been spoken of in the book of Malachi. The picture emerging from this book indicates that the New Exodus which Second Isaiah had proclaimed has taken place, but has not yet reached the dimensions of the ideal he spoke of. Israel has returned from exile and the Temple services have been restored. Indeed, the priests seem to have grown weary of the performance of them, for irregularities and neglect have crept in. Some of the community have married foreign wives and slackness in the payment of dues is complained of. The reforming work of Ezra and Nehemiah (444 B.C.) seems to still lie in the future.

The people are saying that Yahweh is indifferent to what is right and that he is not a God of justice. The prophet Malachi proclaimed that they would learn the truth when the Lord comes for judgment and appears like a refiner's fire. But before the Lord comes he will send his messenger before him to prepare the way. "Behold, I send my messenger to prepare the way before me, and the Lord whom you seek will suddenly come to his temple" (3:1).

The messenger is described as a messenger of the covenant. He is probably to be connected, at least indirectly, with a passage in the preceding chapter where the priest is spoken of as a messenger of the Lord of hosts. "For the lips of a priest should guard knowledge, and men should seek instruction from his mouth, for he is the messenger of the Lord of hosts" (2:7). Above all, the thought and imagery here are to be connected with that angel of the desert period who guided Israel from Sinai to Canaan. The Lord had declared: "Behold, I send an angel before you, to guard you on the way and to bring you to the place which I have prepared. Give heed to him and hearken to his voice, do not rebel against him, for he will not pardon your transgression; for my name is in him" (Exod. 23:20). Israel is to obey the angel who is Yahweh's ambassador, though (like the angel of the burning bush) he is not distinct from him. "For my name is in him."

It is especially interesting to note that in the same third chapter of Malachi this messenger is identified with the prophet Elijah: "Behold, I will send you Elijah the prophet before the great and terrible day of the Lord comes. And he will turn the hearts of fathers to their children and the hearts of children to their

fathers, lest I come and smite the land with a curse" (4:5-6).
This identification has interesting reverberations in the New Testament.

PRELUDE TO THE NEW EXODUS

John's coming is also the immediate prelude to the definitive fulfillment of the hopes expressed in Second Isaiah for a New Exodus — that a way back to a true life with God would be prepared. At the head of the Book of Consolation we read: "A voice cries: 'In the wilderness prepare the way of the Lord, make straight in the desert a highway for our God'" (Is. 40:3). Accordingly Mark writes at the head of his Gospel: "As it is written in the prophets, 'Behold, I send my messenger before thy face, who shall prepare thy way; the voice of one crying in the wilderness: Prepare the way of the Lord, make his paths straight' — John the baptizer appeared in the wilderness, preaching a baptism of repentance for the forgiveness of sins" (1:2-4).

John is the Lord's messenger spoken of by Malachi. And Malachi spoke of this messenger in terms which recall the Lord's angel who guided the Israelites in the desert, and he identified him with Elijah as well. John is the voice in the wilderness of Second Isaiah. His coming is the announcement that the age of salvation has arrived.

The evangelist St. Mark manages to bring out the meaning of John's coming in a number of other, subtle ways. A number of allusions suggest John the Baptist as Elijah Returned to the knowing reader. St. Mark records that "John was clothed with camel's hair, and had a leather girdle around his waist" (v. 6). This further links John the Baptist with Elijah the Tishbite. The book of Kings relates that King Ahaziah of Israel, successor of Ahab and Jezebel, suffered a fall and lay sick. He sent messengers to inquire at a Canaanite shrine whether he would recover. On their way to the shrine the messengers were met by Elijah, who told them to return to their master and tell him that he was to die for his act of infidelity. Ahaziah asked: "'What kind of man was he who came to meet you and told you these things?' They answered him, 'He wore a garment of haircloth, with a girdle of leather about his loins.' And he said, 'It is Elijah the Tishbite'" (2 Kings 1:7-8).

NEW OUTPOURING OF THE SPIRIT

It was an interesting set of circumstances that led to the emergence of the practice of connecting a reappearance of the prophet Elijah with the beginning of messianic times. In postexilic times, prophecy died out in Israel. The authority of the ancient prophets' writings took the place of the spoken prophetic word. The prophetic gift was seen more and more as an eschatological phenomenon which would become a reality again only at the end of days. "As a result of his absence at that time, the Spirit was looked upon in Judaism as an eschatological element. There had been prophets in the past, and there would be prophets again at the end of days. Thus prophecy became more and more the subject of eschatological expectation." [13]

At times this general expectation took the form of an expectation that a prophet would appear at the end who would be the fulfillment, so to speak, of all earlier prophecy. Indeed, since all the prophets had proclaimed basically the same divine truth, the idea arose that the same prophet was successively incarnated in different men, that actually the same prophet always appeared, each time merely taking a different form.

The book of Deuteronomy represents Moses as saying: "The Lord your God will raise up for you a prophet like me from among you" (18:15). On the basis of this text, belief in the return of Moses himself arose. Others came to believe that it was Elijah or Enoch who was to return. This is understandable since, according to the Old Testament, both had been taken up directly to heaven without dying. Above all, however, the return of Elijah was expected.

The prophet Malachi had foretold that the Lord would send his messenger to prepare the way before him (3:1). Later in the same book Elijah is identified with this messenger: "Behold, I will send you Elijah the prophet before the great and terrible day of the Lord comes. And he will turn the hearts of fathers to their children and the hearts of children to their fathers, lest I come and smite the land with a curse" (4:5-6). In the book of Jesus ben Sira the returned Elijah shares with the Suffering Servant the task of restoring the tribes of Israel (Sir. 48:10-11). Against this background Mark's application of Malachi's messen-

[13] O. Cullmann, *Christology of the New Testament*, 14f.

ger passage to John the Baptist takes on great meaning. "The very appearance of John the Baptist was considered an eschatological event. Here again appears a living prophet like the ancient prophets. Probably his baptizing also was widely understood as a prophetic act of the same kind as the symbolic deeds undertaken by Old Testament prophets in particular situations — deeds like those of Jeremiah, Elijah, Elisha, Isaiah, and especially Ezekiel."[14]

JOHN'S BAPTISM

But there was something more here than the symbolic deeds undertaken by the Old Testament prophets. The very fact that John was given the title Baptist is probably an indication of the novelty of his procedure. "The baptism of proselytes, practised by the Jewish community, must be viewed as mere ceremonial cleansing without sacramental meaning; it is found at the end of the first century, but probably was older. The texts of Qumran (the Dead Sea Scrolls) give further insight into ceremonial washings, also non-sacramental. As far as we know, John was the first to employ baptism as a means of religious purification promising forgiveness of sin and an initiation into the eschatological congregation of God. But, according to the gospel record, John himself recognized the incomplete and provisional character of the baptism administered by him: 'I have baptized you with water; but he will baptize you with the Holy Spirit' (Mark 1:8)."[15]

Furthermore, by John's baptism of repentance for the forgiveness of sins in the setting that Mark gives it by association with Malachi, Isaiah, and Elijah, we are to understand that it was related in imagery to the crossing of the Red Sea under Moses. St. Paul reminds his converts at Corinth that, "our fathers . . . all passed through the sea, and all were baptized with Moses in the cloud and in the sea" (1 Cor. 10:1-2). Calling upon the Jews to repent of their past, to confess their sins, to be baptized, John was inviting them to enter the New Israel. He was profoundly convinced that there was about to come among them one who would give the reality of which his baptism was still only a symbol.

[14] *Ibid.*, 15.
[15] J. Hastings, *Dictionary of the Bible*, 87.

Jesus' coming forth from the water of the Jordan evokes the idea of the Hebrews coming forth from the waters of the Red Sea, an experience which formed them into the people of God. In this instance, Jesus, the one, represents the many. Already in his time the prophet Hosea had recorded an oracle in which the Lord hearkens back to the origin of his people. The Lord declares: "When Israel was a child, I loved him, and out of Egypt I called my son" (11:1). Now at Jesus' baptism the voice from heaven declares: "Thou art my beloved son; with thee I am well pleased."

In the Exodus imagery context this means that in Jesus God sees the beginning of the life of his New People. The words from heaven evoke two of the most profound themes of the Old Testament preparation. "Thou art my beloved son" bespeaks the ordination formula of the messianic king of Israel, sending us as it does to Psalm 2 ("You are my son, today I have begotten you" (v. 7). The phrase "with thee I am well pleased" evokes the profound theology of the Suffering Servant poems of Second Isaiah. And it is generally recognized that in the course of these poems the Suffering Servant shifts from a collective to an individual figure. It is also clear that a collective sense is also an essential element in the Son of Man title which figured so prominently in Jesus' presentation of himself. "Jesus is, from the beginning of the Gospel, more than a *mere* individual; he is the new people of God, its life and its reality. The 'pleasure' of God is a figure derived from the first of the Servant Songs, and surely indicates that the life of the new 'Son' or 'people' of God would, like that of the servant in Isaiah, attain its victorious felicity only through suffering and death."[16]

ST. MATTHEW
BOOK OF THE GENEALOGY

St. Matthew does not begin his Gospel with the preaching of John the Baptist as St. Mark does. St. Matthew carries the story back into Jesus' infancy, in his first two chapters, which seem to be largely of his own composition. Here Matthew's fundamental interest is the fulfillment of prophecy. He wants to show how the historical circumstances of Jesus' birth and infancy may be

[16] J. Marsh, *op. cit.*, 759.

related to Old Testament oracles. It might be said that Matthew 1 and 2 are "very largely made up out of reflections upon certain Old Testament passages read in the light of Jewish expectations and the Christian faith."[17]

In chapters 1 and 2 Matthew compares the beginning of the Gospel account with the early part of the Old Testament, and with emphasis on precisely the Exodus theme. Matthew entitles his book "The book of the genealogy (*genesis*) of Jesus Christ, the son of David, the son of Abraham" (1:1). In this context *genesis* can take on wonderfully manifold meanings. It can mean genealogy or birth; it is the title of the first book in the Old Testament, the book of generations (Gen. 2:4; 5:1).

"The title is therefore telescopic: it can be extended to include more and more of what Matthew is beginning to write about."[18] It can cover only the genealogy which immediately follows (1:1-17), or it can be extended to include the account of Jesus' birth. The same word (*genesis*) is translated "birth" in 1:18: "Now the birth of Jesus Christ took place in this way." Finally, *genesis* can be taken to mean "history" or "life-story," and this could be thought of as referring to the whole new creation which begins at Jesus' conception and will be completed at his second coming. Matthew points out in his first verse that this is the book of the genealogy of Jesus, who is not only the son of Abraham, the son of David, but also the Christ.

Although Mark does not have an infancy narrative, his first verse may well have suggested to Matthew how to begin his Gospel. Mark's opening verse reads: "The beginning (*arche*) of the gospel of Jesus Christ, the son of God." The first verse of Genesis, the first verse of the Bible, reads: "In the beginning (*arche*) God created the heavens and the earth." There are other allusions to Genesis in Mark's first chapter. Thus the Spirit descends over the waters of the Jordan as in Genesis "the Spirit of God was moving over the face of the waters" (1:2).

THE NEW MOSES

St. Matthew's second chapter relates the visit of the wise men, King Herod's atrocities, the flight to Egypt, and the return to

---

[17] J. Fenton, *Gospel of St. Matthew*, 34.
[18] *Ibid.*, 36.

Nazareth, with the Exodus theme serving as the unifying bond. "The Jews looked back to the Exodus from Egypt as the beginning of their history, and looked forward to a new Exodus, under a new Moses, at the end of the world. So the Christians said that Jesus was the new Moses; and in this chapter we shall find a number of places where there are references back to Exodus, and to the birth and early history of Moses."[19]

Jesus is born at Bethlehem as foretold by the prophet Micah. Troubled by the report that a "king of the Jews" had been born, King Herod plots Jesus' death. In the Old Testament the Pharaoh became the symbol of unbelief and hardheartedness, and King Herod plays the role of the Second Pharaoh in the New Exodus. Joseph is warned that Herod is about to search for the child to destroy him and so Joseph must take him to Egypt. "Matthew sees in this a repetition of the events which happened before the Exodus: once more a king is killing Jewish children; but just as Moses had been hidden and saved, so now Jesus is to be saved by flight; and God's purpose will be fulfilled, because he will call his son out of Egypt."[20]

Warned by an angel, Joseph "took the child and his mother by night, and departed (*anechoresen*) to Egypt" (v. 14). In the book of Exodus we read that after Moses had killed the Egyptian whom he had seen beating a Hebrew, the Pharaoh heard of it and sought to kill him. "But Moses fled (*anechoresen* in the LXX) from Pharaoh, and stayed in the land of Midian" (Exod. 2:15). So too, when Herod died, the angel tells Joseph: "Rise, take the child and his mother, and go to the land of Israel, for those who sought the child's life are dead" (v. 20). This is a free quotation from the Lord's instruction to Moses: "Go back to Egypt; for all the men who were seeking your life are dead" (Exod. 4:19).

"Just as, when Pharaoh died, Moses was told to return to Egypt, so now that Herod is dead, Joseph is told to bring Jesus back to Israel; but not to Judea, because one of Herod's sons is king there; he goes to Galilee, to Nazareth; and here again prophecy is fulfilled. . . . Notice the contrast between the Old Testament and the New: in Exodus, the king of Egypt is the enemy of Israel; here, a king of Jerusalem is the enemy. In Exodus, Moses flees for

---

19 *Ibid.*, 44.
20 *Ibid.*, 48.

safety out of Egypt and then returns; here, Jesus is taken into Egypt for safety and then returns. In the Old Testament, Egypt and Pharaoh are the symbols for unbelief and hardness of heart; in the New Testament, Jerusalem and Herod fulfil this role."[21]

From chapter 3 on, St. Matthew is reworking Mark's material (Matthew 3:1–4:17 is his revision of Mark 1:2-15). By additions, especially the longer account of Jesus' temptation in the wilderness, Matthew brings the Exodus theme into great prominence. In his chapters 1 and 2 Matthew compared the beginning of the Gospel narrative with the early parts of the Old Testament, and in particular, the life of Jesus with the life of Moses. Matthew sees this pattern continued in Jesus' baptism at John's hands. "Israel came out of Egypt to the Red Sea where, to quote Paul, they were *all baptized into Moses in the cloud and in the sea* (1 Cor. 10:2). Jesus coming now to John to be baptized by him in the Jordan fulfils the pattern of events foreshadowed in the history of Israel."[22]

In his first two chapters, Matthew has already given the reader some understanding of the person of Jesus, and the baptism account adds to this understanding. Matthew had declared that Jesus was taken to Egypt to fulfill the prophecy: "Out of Egypt have I called my son" (2:15). Jesus' baptism is this new crossing of the Red Sea.

MARK AND MATTHEW
EXODUS INTO WILDERNESS

After Israel's exodus from Egypt, she was led out into the wilderness of Sinai. There she had to undergo forty years of trial and temptation, but these were also forty years during which she enjoyed the Lord's special guidance and protection. After the New Exodus is realized in Jordan's waters, Jesus, who embodies the New People of God, is "led up by the Spirit into the wilderness to be tempted by the devil" (Matthew 4:1). The temptation is given an emphatic theological meaning by its position in the Gospels. St. Mark relates the incident very baldly, yet manages to make the incident say a great deal about one of his special interests — the Wilderness theme as such. By his additions St.

---

[21] *Ibid.*, 50.
[22] *Ibid.*, 58f.

Matthew has turned the passage into a remarkable exposition of the Exodus theme.

Mark says that Jesus was in the wilderness for forty days, tempted by the devil. Matthew nudges the memory to recall Israel's forty years in the desert by writing that Jesus "fasted forty days and forty nights" (4:2). Further, the book of Exodus relates that after Aaron had made the golden calf and Moses broke the stone tablets at the foot of the mountain, Moses was instructed to cut two new tablets and to reascend Mount Sinai. There the covenant is renewed and the text goes on to say that Moses, "was there with the Lord forty days and forty nights; he neither ate bread nor drank water" (34:28).

After Jesus' fast of forty days and forty nights, the tempter came and suggested that he command stones to become loaves of bread. But Jesus answered: "It is written, 'Men shall not live by bread alone, but by every word that proceeds from the mouth of God'" (v. 4). Up to this point Matthew has recorded only one of Jesus' sayings. When John the Baptist showed reluctance to baptize him, Jesus declared: "Let it be so now; for thus it is fitting for us to fulfil all righteousness" (3:15). "*Righteousness (dikaiosyne)* seems to be used here in the sense of the divine commandments; and because these are contained in the Old Testament, to *fulfil all righteousness* is almost equivalent to 'to fulfil the scriptures' — i.e., the baptism in the Red Sea is repeated in the baptism by John in the Jordan."[23]

This pattern is continued in the temptation scene. Jesus speaks three times in the course of this passage and in each case he uses the phrase "it is written," i.e., in the Old Testament. Jesus answers the devil's suggestions by means of references to the Scriptures he has come to fulfil. Jesus' three answers to the devil include quotations which are all from the same book in the Old Testament, Deuteronomy. They all refer to the testing of Israel in the wilderness, after the crossing of the Red Sea. If therefore Matthew had that crossing in mind when he wrote his description of Jesus' baptism by John (3:13-17), he may also have had in mind these events in the wilderness which Deuteronomy describes when he wrote his description of Jesus' temptation in the wilderness.

One Deuteronomy passage in particular seems to be reflected

[23] *Ibid.*, 59.

at the beginning of Matthew's temptation scene. Moses is address-
ing Israel and he says: "And you shall remember all the way
which the Lord your God has led you these forty years in the
wilderness, that he might humble you, testing (*peirazo* in the
LXX) you to know what was in your heart, whether you would
keep his commandments, or not" (8:2). Furthermore, Jesus' answer to the tempter's first suggestion comes from the very next
verse (Deut. 8:3). Similarly Jesus "was led up by the Spirit, into
the wilderness, to be tempted (*peirazo*) and he fasted forty days
and forty nights" (Matthew 4:1). "It may therefore be that we
are to see here that Jesus fulfils the role of Israel, passing through
similar temptations and testings; but where Israel had failed,
Jesus is triumphant."[24]

Against the background of the New Exodus, Jesus necessarily
stands forth as the New Moses and for Matthew's purposes the
gospel may be regarded as the New Law of the Lord which receives its promulgation in the Sermon on the Mount. In the Old
Testament we see Israel crossing the Red Sea, traveling through
the wilderness to Mount Sinai, where the Lord promulgates his
Law and the covenant is formed. So in the New Testament, Jesus
is baptized (New Exodus), is in the desert for forty days (wilderness period), and then goes to the mountain in Galilee to proclaim the New Law of the Kingdom of God.

FIRST TEMPTATION — WILDERNESS OF SIN

When the tempter suggests that he command stones to become
loaves of bread, Jesus answers: "It is written, 'Man shall not live
by bread alone, but by every word that proceeds from the mouth
of God'" (4:4).

The Israelites were not many days out of Egypt when they
began to doubt the Lord's power to provide. When the people
of Israel came to the wilderness of Sin, "the whole congregation
of the people of Israel murmured against Moses and Aaron in
the wilderness, and said to them, 'Would that we had died by the
hand of the Lord in the land of Egypt, when we sat by the flesh-
pots and ate bread to the full; for you have brought us out into
this wilderness to kill this whole assembly with hunger'" (Exod.

---

[24] *Ibid.*, 62.

16:2-4). And the book of Deuteronomy shows Moses at the end of his life thinking back over the desert period. He reminds Israel that the Lord, "humbled you and let you hunger and fed you with manna, which you did not know, nor did your fathers know; that he might make you know that man does not live by bread alone, but that man lives by everything that proceeds out of the mouth of the Lord" (8:3). It is from this verse that Jesus' first answer to Satan comes.

At the close of the baptism scene the voice from heaven was heard to declare: "This is my beloved Son, with whom I am well pleased" (3:17). As portrayed by Matthew the following temptation scene stands forth as an attempt on Satan's part to induce Jesus to act contrary to his vocation as the perfectly obedient Son of God. Pierre Bonnard writes in a recent commentary on Matthew: "Satan attempts to turn Jesus aside from his vocation as an obedient son by inviting him to utilize his authority as Son for his own advantage. More exactly and simply: Satan invites Jesus to supply his own existence and no longer to count exclusively on his father."[25]

SECOND TEMPTATION — REPHIDIM

After Jesus' first temptation, Matthew tells us that "the devil took him to the holy city, and set him on the pinnacle of the temple, and said to him, 'If you are the Son of God, throw yourself down; for it is written,

"He will give his angels charge of you,"

and

"On their hands they will bear you up,
    lest you strike your foot against a stone."'

Jesus said to him, 'Again it is written, "You shall not tempt the Lord your God"'" (4:5-7).

In their exodus wanderings the Hebrews moved from the wilderness of Sin to Rephidim. Jesus' first reply to Satan was connected with the former; his second reply is connected with the latter.

The book of Exodus tells us that "all the congregation of the people of Israel moved on from the wilderness of Sin by stages,

[25] *L'Evangile selon Saint Matthieu*, 44.

according to the commandment of the Lord, and camped at Rephidim; but there was no water for the people to drink. Therefore the people found fault with Moses, and said, 'Give us water to drink.' And Moses said to them, 'Why do you find fault with me? Why do you put the Lord to the proof?' But the people thirsted there for water, and the people murmured against Moses, and said, 'Why did you bring us up out of Egypt, to kill us and our children and our cattle with thirst?' So Moses cried to the Lord, 'What shall I do with this people? They are almost ready to stone me.' And the Lord said to Moses, 'Pass on before the people, taking with you some of the elders of Israel; and take in your hand the rod with which you struck the Nile, and go. Behold, I will stand before you there on the rock at Horeb; and you shall strike the rock, and water shall come out of it, that the people may drink.' And Moses did so, in the sight of the elders of Israel. And he called the name of the place Massah (Proof) and Meribah (Contention), because of the faultfinding of the children of Israel, and because they put the Lord to the proof by saying, 'Is the Lord among us or not?'" (Exod. 17:1-7).

Again, in the book of Deuteronomy we hear Moses reflecting on this incident from the wilderness years, and he admonishes the people: "You shall not put the Lord your God to the test, as you tested him at Massah" (6:16). It is from this verse that Jesus draws his reply to Satan's second suggestion — that, trusting in his Father's protection, he should throw himself down from the pinnacle of the Temple. Satan quotes Psalm 91 in support of his suggestion: "He will give his angels charge of you . . . on their hands they will bear you up, lest you strike your foot against a stone" (Matthew 4:6).

Here Pierre Bonnard comments: "Satan chose his text well, for Jesus himself belonged to the 'poor of the Lord' who for a long time had used such psalms to express their confidence in distress. . . . Satan uses Psalm 91 in a literalistic way; Jesus replies with what we today would call theological exegesis. While it is good to have confidence in God, it is also necessary that this confidence not disguise a secret, or even unconscious intention to use God's power to further man's religious ambition. Is Satan proposing to Jesus that he work a miracle before the temple crowd to immediately accredit himself as the Messiah? Probably not; he seeks rather to detach Jesus from filial obedience to the Father and lead him to assume an autonomous consciousness of his powers as son. In the context of Deut. 6:16 the theme of the temptation of the Lord perhaps has a slightly different meaning. It means: to disobey the Lord to see how far his patience will go. The contrary of this putting to test is expressed in v. 17: 'you shall diligently keep the commandments of the Lord your God.' In our text Satan would not be proposing an action evil in itself; it would be evil only if it were placed at the service of a usurped and autonomous messianism." [26]

THIRD TEMPTATION — WILDERNESS OF SINAI

"Again, the devil took him to a very high mountain, and showed him all the kingdoms of the world and the glory of them; and he said to him, 'All these I will give you, if you will fall down and worship me.' Then Jesus said to him, 'Begone, Satan! for it is written,

> "You shall worship the Lord your God
> and him only shall you serve."'

Then the devil left him, and behold, angels came and ministered to him" (Matthew 4:7-11).

On the third new moon after leaving Egypt the people of Israel came to the wilderness of Sinai and encamped before the mountain. And when Moses delayed to come down from the mountain the people came to Aaron and said: "Up, make us gods, who shall go before us" (Exod. 32:1). And Aaron took their gold and fashioned a molten calf and the people worshipped it and sacrificed to it. They cried out: "These are our gods, who brought us up out of the land of Egypt" (Exod. 32:10).

Moses reflects on this incident as well, at his life's end, and we hear him admonishing the Israelites: "You shall fear the Lord your God; you shall serve him, and swear by his name. You shall not go after other gods, of the gods of the peoples who are round about you; for the Lord your God in the midst of you is a jealous God; lest the anger of the Lord your God be kindled against you,

[26] *Ibid.*, 45.

and he destroy you from off the face of the earth" (Deut. 6:13-15).

Jesus does not commit the sin of Israel in worshipping other gods; and he therefore receives what the devil had (falsely) promised him, and more. At the end of his Gospel Matthew relates how the risen Savior appeared to the apostles in Galilee and declared: "All authority in heaven and on earth has been given to me. Go therefore and make disciples of all nations" (28:18-19).

Jesus' answer to this third temptation begins with the exclamation: "Begone, Satan!" These words are found in another context (Mark 8:33=Matthew 16:23), where they are addressed to Peter after he had tempted Jesus to avoid crucifixion at Jerusalem "There may be more than a verbal link between these passages: the temptations of the devil here are temptations to live in a way different from that of faith in God and obedience to his commandments. Jesus rejects the tempter both here and later in chapter 16; he goes to Jerusalem, and suffers, and dies, and is raised from the dead, and is rewarded with all authority."[27] One is also reminded of the great Christological hymn: "He humbled himself and became obedient unto death, even death on a cross. Therefore God has exalted him and bestowed on him the name which is above every name" (Phil. 2:8-9).

Satan begins the first two temptations with the condition: "If you are the Son of God." This phrase links the temptations with Matthew's account of the crucifixion where the title "Son of God" is prominent. Thus the passersby jeer: "If you are the Son of God, come down from the cross. . . . He trusts in God; let God deliver him now, if he desires him; for he said, 'I am the Son of God'" (27:40, 43). "Jesus is confronted with a sharp alternative: power or filial service. . . . The question put to Jesus is this: is he going to fulfill his mission in filial humility or in 'messianic' glory in the political, Zealot sense, as found for example in the Psalms of Solomon (chapter 17)?"[28]

The temptation, therefore, has deep religious meaning by its position in the Gospels. As Matthew notes, the Lord has called his Son out of Egypt (2:15). Like the old Israel after the Exodus,

---

[27] Fenton, *op. cit.*, 64f.
[28] Bonnard, *op. cit.*, 46.

the New Son is tested in the wilderness, the forty days being some equivalence in imagery for the former forty years. And after the temptation, Jesus returns to Galilee and begins to preach the Kingdom. "Jesus came into Galilee, preaching the gospel of God, and saying, 'The time is fulfilled, and the kingdom of God is at hand'" (1:14).

What has gone before has shown that in Christ the life of the New Israel has begun. Now it is made clear that the "good news is proclaimed as the beginning, not of a series of individual re-actions, but of a realm or divine kingdom. What has begun, in Mark's view, is neither the merely individual life of a founder of a new religion, nor the mere beginning of a new society; it is both in one, and the Kingdom is proclaimed because the Christ is there, and the Christ is there since God has acted to re-create his people in his Son."[29]

PUBLIC LIFE — SERMON ON THE MOUNT

Jesus went about Galilee, teaching in the synagogues and preaching the gospel of the Kingdom and healing the sick and infirm. Soon great crowds began to follow him. And "seeing the crowds," St. Matthew writes, Jesus "went up on the mountain, and when he sat down his disciples came to him. And he opened his mouth and taught them" (5:1). The reader is not told which mountain, and he does not need to be, because he has been pre-pared for this since the infancy narrative. There Matthew showed us a wicked king again killing Hebrew children and Jesus being taken to Egypt. As Matthew points out: "This was to fulfil what the Lord had spoken by the prophet, 'Out of Egypt have I called my son'" (2:15). Jesus is the fulfillment of Moses, the Second Moses.

If this parallel is to be completed, there must be a progression to a mountain, the formation of a New Covenant, and the giving of a New Law. So after the first phase of Galilean activity, Jesus, who embodies the New People, goes to the mountain and pro-claims the Law of the Kingdom. "Just as Moses received the Law from God on the mountain in the Old Testament, so Jesus gives his teaching to the disciples on the mountain. The comparison

[29] J. Marsh, *op. cit.*, 749.

and contrast between the Law which was given to Moses and the commandments of Jesus runs through much of the following section."[30]

This section, the Sermon on the Mount, is the first of five discourse sections which all end with the formula for transition from teaching to narrative. Matthew intended to see in the teaching of this first discourse that which, in the Christian faith, corresponds to the Law in the Old Testament. "In Exodus there is a description of the making of the covenant between God and Israel: Moses *took the book* of the covenant, and read it in the hearing of the people; and they said, All that the Lord has spoken we will do, and we will be obedient. And Moses took the blood and threw it upon the people, and said, Behold the blood of the covenant which the Lord has made with you in accordance with *all these words* (Exod. 24:7f). Jesus has come to make a new covenant with a new Israel: cf. 26:28 *this is my* blood of the covenant, which is poured out for many for the *forgiveness* of sins. His death corresponds to the blood of oxen in Exod. 24; his commandments correspond to the words of the Lord there — i.e., to the Law."[31] Sharp contrasts between the Law and Jesus' teaching appear repeatedly in the remainder of the sermon: "You have heard that it was said . . . but I say to you" (5:21, 27, 31, 33, 38, 43). Since, in the eyes of the Pharisees, there was nothing holier than the Law, nothing could have been more radical than Jesus' putting himself above their extensions and applications of Mosaic Law.

THE APOSTLES

Jesus' withdrawal to the mountain is followed by his selection of the twelve apostles. As Mark writes, Jesus "went up into the hills, and called to him those whom he desired; and they came to him. And he appointed twelve, to be with him, and to be sent out to preach and have authority to cast out demons" (3:13-15).

Locating the specific mountain is not the first consideration. A mountain is the traditional setting for a solemn divine act. So Jesus climbs a mountain and chooses from all Israel gathered together, the foundation members of the eschatological community.

[30] Fenton, *op. cit.*, 77.
[31] *Ibid.*, 77f.

In Mark the calling of Peter and Andrew, James and John comes immediately after Jesus' baptism. Jesus said: "Follow me . . . and immediately they left their nets and followed him" (1:17-18). "Follow" (*akoloutheo*) is the word that Christians generally used for the acceptance of Jesus' call and attachment to his person. Here we see what such following must always be like. "Jesus' demands brook no delay (*immediately*); the response must be decisive and must include willingness to give up one's means of livelihood and make a clean break with one's past." [32]

So likewise when Jesus appoints the Twelve (Mark 3:13-15), Jesus' word is with power and those who are chosen obey the summons without more ado. They are the new Israel, and since the old Israel, as God originally formed it, was a twelve-fold body, the new Israel is conceived in the same way and is accordingly provided with twelve leaders. "There is little room for doubt that this act was intended to be a manifest sign of the formation and presence of a new Israel, where Jesus had the place of Yahweh and the Twelve took the place of the Patriarchs and/or their tribes." [33]

JESUS FEEDS FIVE THOUSAND

After Jesus had appointed the Twelve, he taught the multitudes by the Sea of Galilee by means of parables and performed a number of miracles. Then he sent out the Twelve on a preaching and healing mission (Mark 3:7–6:13). Afterwards "the apostles returned to Jesus, and told him all that they had done and taught. And he said to them, 'Come away by yourselves to a lonely place, and rest a while'" (Mark 6:30-31). Jesus and the apostles set out for their retreat by boat. But they had been observed. People ran there on foot from all the towns, and got there ahead of them. And as Jesus "landed he saw a great throng, and he had compassion on them, because they were like sheep without a shepherd; and he began to teach them many things" (6:34). And when it grew late, Jesus "commanded them all to sit down by companies upon the green grass. So they sat down in groups, by hundreds and by fifties. And taking the five loaves and the two fish he looked up to heaven, and blessed, and broke the loaves, and gave

[32] D. E. Nineham, *Gospel of St. Mark*, 72.
[33] Marsh, *op. cit.*, 760.

them to the disciples to set before the people; and he divided the two fish among them all. And they all ate and were satisfied. And they took up twelve baskets full of broken pieces and of the fish. And those who ate the loaves were five thousand men" (Mark 6:39-44).

In his article "The Theology of the New Testament" in *Peake's Commentary*, John Marsh brings out the meaning of this passage in a striking way. "What is clear, looking back to the past," he writes, "is that in a lonely place the new leader or shepherd of the pilgrim people of God fed the newly pledged new Israel with miraculous food, as Moses had done before him. What is clear, looking forward to the future, is that the evangelist could not write of that meal (or of the meal with the four thousand) save in manifest Eucharistic terms: 'Taking the . . . loaves . . . he looked up to heaven, and blessed, and broke . . . and gave . . .' (Mark 6:41; cf. 8:6). But again, in the eloquent reserve of the evangelist, the difference between the 'new Moses' and the old is significant, though not stridently accented: Moses was not himself the feeder of Israel in the desert, and even though the manna prefigured the Eucharist, it was in essence food for the body; but Jesus was himself the feeder of the new Israel in the lonely place, and though the food was for physical satisfaction, its main significance was as the prefiguring of the Eucharist where the physical is made so overwhelmingly the vehicle of the spiritual" (76of).

THE TRANSFIGURATION

After the feeding of the five thousand, Jesus continues his ministry of preaching and healing. He moves out to the edges of Canaan, to the region of Tyre and Sidon and to Caesarea Philippi. There Peter declares: "You are the Christ," and Jesus speaks even more clearly and emphatically of the necessity for him to suffer and of the necessity for his followers to walk in the same path. Then, as reported by Mark, "after six days Jesus took with him Peter and James and John, and led them up a high mountain apart by themselves; and he was transfigured before them, and his garments became glistening, intensely white, as no fuller on earth could bleach them. And there appeared to them Elijah with Moses; and they were talking to Jesus" (Mark 9:2-4).

If we wish to sum up the overall meaning of the Transfiguration, we can probably not do better than to say with Professor Marsh that the incident shows that "the Jesus of history was always the glorified Christ of faith, and that the glorified Christ of faith is none other than the Jesus of history."[34] But this point is made by a striking use of the Exodus theme. It unites most aspects of the Exodus theme we have met up to this point. Moses and Elijah represent the Law and the Prophets and their presence is the witness of the Old Covenant to its own fulfillment. Moses and Elijah are both wilderness prophets and under this aspect their very presence is a sign that Jesus is the Messiah. We have seen how Elijah was associated with the coming of the Messiah from the time of Malachi and how he became the eschatological prophet *par excellence*. Yet belief in the return of Moses was current among the Samaritans. Moses' prophecy that the Lord would raise up a prophet like him (Deut. 18:15) was an important text for the members of the Dead Sea community.

While Peter puts Jesus still on the same level as Moses and Elijah, the voice marks the uniqueness of the Son: "This is my beloved Son; listen to him." The cloud occurs as the symbol of the divine presence in the theophanies of the Exodus and at the dedication of the first Temple; it was expected to reappear in messianic times. The second book of Maccabees records the tradition that when Jeremiah hid the tent, the ark, and the altar of incense after the destruction of the Temple, he declared: "The place shall be unknown until God gathers his people together again and shows his mercy. And then the Lord will disclose these things, and the glory of the Lord and the cloud will appear" (2:7-8).

In the New Testament the cloud is connected with the Transfiguration, the Ascension, and the Parousia. Mark appears to think of it as the vehicle of God's presence, the abode of his glory, from which he speaks. The voice from the cloud echoes the words spoken at the baptism (Mark 1:11), with the addition of "listen to him" from Deuteronomy 18:15 — the prophet like unto Moses is identified with the Christ, the beloved Son.

Peter's desire to build three booths is of particular interest. It is evident that Mark considered them an inappropriate response

[34] *Op. cit.*, 761.

to the situation: "he did not know what to say" (Mark 9:6). Peter's words seem to express a desire on his part to prolong the blessedness of the experience, when in fact it was God's will for Christ and the disciples that they should return into the world and enter upon the path of suffering. The pericope ends with the statement that "suddenly looking around they no longer saw any one with them but Jesus only" (v. 8). The conditions of the Transfiguration pass completely and abruptly. The cloud and the two heavenly figures disappear, and Jesus stands among the disciples once more a man among men.

Mark is here exploiting a particular aspect of contemporary Jewish eschatological expectation. The day of salvation, the day of the Lord, was often pictured as a day when God would once more "pitch his tent" with his people as he had done during the forty years in the wilderness. The Jewish Feast of Tabernacles itself had acquired an eschatological significance, not only looking back to the tent-dwelling of the wilderness days but also forward to the new age when God would again "tabernacle" with his people, and members of all nations would gather in Jerusalem to "tabernacle" there and worship God together. St. John also uses this aspect of Jewish eschatological thought as we shall see at some length further on. Chapters 6 and 7 of John are set against the background of the Feast of Tabernacles and not a little of the meaning of these chapters follows from this circumstance.

The image of tent-dwelling in thought about the new age is found elsewhere in the New Testament. St. Paul writes to the Corinthians: "We know that if the earthly tent is destroyed, we have a building from God" (2 Cor. 5:1). In Apocalypse the seer tells us that he heard a great voice from heaven saying: "Behold, the dwelling of God is with men. He will dwell with them, and they shall be his people, and God himself will be with them" (Apoc. 21:3). "This being so, St. Mark may well have understood Peter's words eschatologically — as an offer to build the sort of dwellings God and Christ were expected to share with men in the age to come. In that case what Peter was overlooking was that this scene was not the parousia, but only its foreshadowing. Before the end, there remained much to be done and much to be suffered both by Jesus and by his disciples (see e.g., chapter

13). That suffering is not to be by-passed or evaded, as Peter here seems to think (cf. his attitude to the prediction of suffering in the previous episode)."[35]

From the vantage point of their superior knowledge, Mark and Luke judge Peter's proposal to build three booths to be ill-considered. But from Peter's viewpoint the proposal was a plausible one. "He saw three men, each one a manifestation of the divine glory, and he wanted to capture the fleeting and stupendous moment by providing for each one a tabernacle such as Israel had built in the wilderness to enshrine the glory of the Lord. Perhaps it confirmed his faith in Jesus to see him in such company: for Moses had spoken with God as a man speaks with his friend, so that his face shone as he received the law at God's hand, and, like Elijah, he had stood alone as the champion of God's people; both men had made such an impression on their fellows that they were believed to have been translated bodily to heaven, and both were regarded as forerunners of the kingdom. What Peter did not realize was that Moses and Elijah belonged, with John the Baptist, to the old order that was passing away, and that a moment later he would see them vanish, leaving Jesus alone, and hear a voice say, 'This is my Son, my Chosen; listen to him!' (cf. Deut. 18:15). There was no need for three tabernacles: the divine glory, imperfectly and partially revealed under the old dispensation, was now being gathered up in the sole person of this Jesus who had set his face to go to Jerusalem. He stood alone, and the cloud of the divine presence overshadowed him and his."[36]

THE TRANSFIGURATION IN LUKE

St. Luke makes some subtle changes and adaptions in his Transfiguration account, and these serve generally to enhance the Exodus theme. Matthew and Mark say that the Transfiguration takes place "after six days," i.e., six days after Jesus' preceding sayings about suffering and glorification. Luke writes: "Now about eight days after these sayings" (9:28). It would seem that Luke's purpose was to indicate the first day of the week and thereby to underline the relation of the Transfiguration to the Resurrection

[35] Nineham, *op. cit.*, 237.
[36] G. B. Caird, *Gospel of St. Luke*, 133.

and to demonstrate the meaning of Jesus' glorification through death. The two prophets' appearance, "in glory," forms another link between his foreshadowing of Christ's glorification and both the Resurrection and the Ascension. As the "prophet like Moses," Jesus is attested by Moses and Elijah, the Lawgiver and the great Prophet, both of whom ascended into heaven.

Mark and Matthew say simply that Moses and Elijah talked to Jesus. Luke tells us what they talked about. "Moses and Elijah appeared in glory and spoke of his *exodus*" (Luke 9:31). Quite clearly Luke wishes to set Jesus' work in his death and resurrection in relation to the great Exodus tradition. "At Jerusalem Jesus was to accomplish the New Exodus, leading God's people from a greater bondage than that of Egypt into the promised land of the kingdom. Like Moses of old, he was now standing on the brink of a great sea, the ocean of iniquity through which he must pass and in which he must accomplish another baptism (12:50). He has always obeyed the Father, but the road he has travelled hitherto has been well marked by the feet of prophets and forerunners, like Moses and Elijah. Now God is about to lead him into a path never before trodden by human foot, a path which will lead him to Gethsemane and Calvary. Henceforth, as pioneer of our salvation (Heb. 2:10; 12:2), he must journey alone, and not even Moses and Elijah can bear him company. Others, indeed, like John the Baptist, have suffered and died in God's service, but the death that awaits this man is more than martyrdom."[37]

Also special to Luke is the notation that it was when "the men were parting from Jesus" (9:33), that Peter spoke to Jesus about making the three booths. This would seem to underline the point which is also made in the other Synoptics. While Moses and Elijah bear witness to Jesus, like John the Baptist they belong to the old order which is passing away. The Voice speaks to Jesus alone and defines his mission as Suffering Servant and Eschatological Prophet.

THE EUCHARIST: THE PASSOVER BACKGROUND

After his transfiguration Jesus continued to speak of his coming passion and death as he and his disciples made their way to

[37] *Ibid.*, 132f.

Jerusalem. Passing through Galilee they came to Capharnaum; they traversed "the region of Judea and beyond the Jordan" (Mark 10:1), and came to Jericho. Then they went up to Jerusalem, where Jesus' predictions of death and resurrection were to be realized.

In their passion narratives both the Synoptics and John stress the connection between Jesus' passion and death and the feast of the Passover, the great Exodus feast. And Jesus' words and actions both in the institution of the Eucharist and through his passion make it clear that this Passover background was central to his thought. Thus at the head of his passion narrative, Mark notes that it was "two days before the Passover and the feast of the Unleavened Bread" (14:1) when the chief priests and scribes determined to put Jesus to death; and the other Synoptics echo him.

It was on the first day of Unleavened Bread, "when they sacrificed the passover lamb," that Jesus instructed his disciples how they were to prepare for the feast. John creates some difficulty here since he follows a different chronology. He is a day ahead of the Synoptics; Jesus dies at the time when the passover lambs were slain in the Temple, when, according to the Synoptics, Jesus and the disciples were preparing for the Last Supper.

However this problem is to be explained, the Passover supper in the Synoptic Gospels is beyond question and it seems no less clear that John too intends the supper and the death to be viewed against the Passover background. Alan Richardson has written: "The symbolism of the bread and the wine come directly from the Jewish passover ceremony, whether the Last Supper itself was or was not a passover meal; the important point to notice is that, as it occurred about passover-time, the early Church interpreted its meaning in terms of Old Testament passover-theology. Jesus had died at passover-time; what could be more significant to a Jewish Christian in the early days of the Church? There is no reason whatever to doubt that Jesus himself had taught this interpretation of his own death or indeed that he had deliberately gone to Jerusalem for the feast of the Passover because he had come to think of himself as 'the Lamb' which God had provided for sacrifice."[38]

[38] A. Richardson, *An Introduction to the Theology of the New Testament*, 370f.

Along the same line, Richardson writes at the head of his consideration of Eucharistic theology in the New Testament: "The fact that from apostolic days the Church has met to break the bread and drink the cup is a continuing testimony to the truth of Jesus's interpretation of the significance of his own death as the means of ratifying a new covenant between God and man."[39] If any justification for St. John's procedure is needed, it may well be pointed out, with Father McKenzie, that "the Passover commemorated the great saving event, the deliverance of Israel from slavery and its constitution as the people of Yahweh; and the Priestly source of the Pentateuch places the first Passover supper in Egypt as an anticipation of the saving event which occurred that night. The new Passover is likewise anticipated by a dinner; and at this dinner the new Passover lamb, whose blood on the doors was a sign of deliverance, is consumed by the disciples, the little core of the New Israel. The Lamb is consumed sacramentally."[40]

THE CHRISTIAN PASSOVER

The Eucharist is so remarkably rich in symbolic significance that it presents almost all the major themes of the primitive Christian preaching and teaching. Amidst this wealth of Eucharistic symbolism, it is not easy to disengage the primary theme. But it appears to be the Eucharist as the Christian Passover. Paul records our Lord's injunction that the Eucharist was to be celebrated "in remembrance of me" (1 Cor. 11:24), and he reminds the same Corinthians: "Christ, our paschal lamb, has been sacrificed" (5:7). Unquestionably the primary meaning of "in remembrance of me" is "to be found in the conception of the Eucharist as the Christian passover-feast."[41] The Passover of the Jews was above all things a memorial of the deliverance of Israel from Egypt at the Exodus. Exodus 12:14 reads: "This day shall be for you a memorial day, and you shall keep it as a feast to the Lord; throughout your generations you shall observe it as an ordinance for ever." The next verse goes on to speak of the Feast of Unleavened Bread, which is later said also to be for a memorial of

[39] *Ibid.*, 365.
[40] J. L. McKenzie, *Dictionary of the Bible*, 250f.
[41] Richardson, *op. cit.*, 370.

"what the Lord did for me when I came out of Egypt" (Exod. 13:8-9).

It is clear, therefore, what St. Paul has in mind when he writes to the Corinthians: "Cleanse out the old leaven that you may be fresh dough, as you really are unleavened. For Christ, our paschal lamb, has been sacrificed. Let us, therefore, celebrate the festival, not with the old leaven" (1 Cor. 5:7-8). When St. Paul records Jesus as bidding his disciples to "do this" in remembrance, he understands that Jesus is instituting a new Passover memorial which commemorates the deliverance of the New Israel from sin and death.

The "this" of Jesus' injunction "must be understood to mean the whole act of Eucharistic worship, including the recital of what the Lord Jesus had done and said on the night on which he was betrayed: it must include the *taking* of bread and of wine, the blessing (or giving of thanks), the *breaking* of the bread and the giving of these elements to be eaten and drunk — the fourfold 'shape' of the liturgy."[42]

The symbolism is quite straightforward. The bread of the Christian Passover is, like the unleavened bread of the Jews, itself a sign and memorial of what God has done for us. It is also the paschal lamb of the Christian Passover feast, the body of Jesus, who is himself the Lamb of God who takes away the sins of the world. The wine is mixed in a cup by itself. The Lamb is slain: the blood is already separated from the body.

The Eucharist is a "memorial," Father McKenzie has written, "in the sense of cultic recital and reenactment of the saving event, by which each participant experiences the event and is personally integrated into the death and resurrection of Jesus, in terms of which Paul often describes the new life of the Christian. . . . The covenant is sealed by sacrifice which symbolizes the bond; Jesus, as the bond of the new covenant through his death, is the victim of the covenant sacrifice."[43]

THE EUCHARIST IN LUKE

It is in Luke that the Last Supper stands forth most clearly as the Christian Passover. When compared with the other Synop-

[42] *Ibid.*, 370.
[43] McKenzie, *op. cit.*, 251.

tics, Luke's version of the institution of the Lord's Supper is seen to have a number of striking peculiarities. Luke begins his account with an explicit affirmation that the meal was a Passover meal. Jesus declares: "I have earnestly desired to eat this passover with you before I suffer; for I tell you I shall not eat it until it is fulfilled in the kingdom of God" (Luke 22:15-16). Mark and Matthew relegate the reference to the eschatological kingdom to the end of their institution accounts.

Then in Luke's account two cups are mentioned. Verse 17 says that Jesus "took a cup"; then "he took bread" (v. 19); and verse 20 goes on to say: "And likewise the cup after supper, saying, 'This cup which is poured out for you is the new covenant in my blood.'" Commentators have too readily marked down Luke's version of the institution to a clumsy conflation and removed verses 19b-20 from their text. Father Pierre Benoit has argued convincingly that in doing so they miss a theological point that Luke makes with great skill.[44]

When they speak of the preparations for the Last Supper, Mark and Matthew make it clear that the Passover was at hand. But when they speak of the institution itself, it is nowhere mentioned that it was a Passover meal. Father Benoit says that there is a good reason for this. In reporting the institution, Mark and Matthew are using a somewhat stylized liturgical formula that the Church had been using for the celebration of the Eucharist. That the Last Supper was a Passover meal does not appear in this liturgical formula. Luke is restoring a theological consideration that was in danger of being lost sight of — that the Eucharist is the Christian Passover. To this end Luke anticipates the mention of the bread and the cup. The bread is implicitly anticipated in the mention of the Passover in verse 15: "I have earnestly desired to *eat* this passover with you"; the cup is mentioned in verse 17. In each case a reference to the eschatological kingdom follows.

As a result of this arrangement, the old rite which is passing away, the Jewish Passover, and the new Eucharistic rite which is replacing it are represented on facing panels. "Jesus bids farewell to the old rite and immediately after institutes the new. By his arrangement, Luke wishes to set forth a profound theological thought which later tradition will develop: the Eucharist is the

---

[44] *Exégèse et Théologie*, I, 163–203.

Christian Pasch; or again, Christ suppressed the old Pasch by substituting himself for it. This is an idea that St. Paul has already advanced (1 Cor. 5:7); we may well believe that Luke is acting under Paul's influence when he sets forth this idea by his skillful reconstruction."[45] "The Passover meal is not bread but the Passover lamb; the Passover lamb of the new Christian Passover is the bread which becomes the body of Christ. Hence the cup of 22:17 is not yet the cup of the Eucharist; it is the Passover cup which becomes the Eucharist."[46]

THE SACRIFICE OF THE SUFFERING SERVANT

As Alan Richardson emphatically states, we must be on our guard against interpreting either the Last Supper or the Christian Eucharist exclusively in terms of the Passover. "Here again we have an obvious illustration of how fatal for our understanding of the Scriptures is the assumption that any particular passage will have only one interpretation."[47]

The Eucharist is also a sacrifice. While the Passover lamb is not clearly a sacrificial animal, Jesus explained the Christian Passover in terms of the vicarious sacrifice of the Suffering Servant of the Lord. Professor Cullmann has pointed out that while the differences between the four versions of Jesus' institution of the Lord's Supper are quite considerable in detail, all four passages agree on the most important point: when Jesus distributed the supper, he announced that he would shed his blood "for many," and this is quite clearly a Suffering Servant allusion. "The very fact that these different reports do not agree in other respects makes this fundamental agreement all the more significant. . . . Moreover, the fact that all four contain the word *diatheke* ("covenant") is also important for our problem, since we have seen that the ideas of *representation* and *covenant* are precisely the two main elements of the work which according to the Old Testament the *'ebed Yahweh* must accomplish. The preposition 'for' or 'instead of,' which is basic to the idea of representation, plays an important part in Is. 53. Is. 42:6 and 49:8 ascribe to the *'ebed* the task of re-establishing the covenant between God and his peo-

---

[45] *Ibid.*, 192.
[46] McKenzie, *op. cit.*, 250.
[47] *Op. cit.*, 371.

ple — in fact, in this context the *'ebed* himself *is* the *berith* in person."[48]

At the Last Supper, therefore, Jesus announced what he would accomplish the next day on the Cross. And Jesus' use of the Suffering Servant theology in the institution of the Eucharist throws light on all the other New Testament passages where this theology appears. By the time the Synoptic Gospels were written, Suffering Servant as a title for Jesus was no longer common in the early Church. "The Gospels prefer other titles for him, above all 'Christ.' It is all the more remarkable that not only Paul but also all three Synoptics in relating the story of the Last Supper recall that Jesus at this decisive moment ascribed to himself the role of the *'ebed Yahweh*."[49]

And other aspects of the institution have a sacrificial background. The cup is interpreted in terms of the "blood of sprinkling" of Exodus 24:8 by which Moses ratified the covenant of Sinai and also in terms of the making of the New Covenant of Jeremiah 31:31. "Jesus regarded his death as the sacrifice by which a new and better covenant was ratified between God and a new Israel, and this is the truth he taught to his disciples when on the night on which he was betrayed he took bread and wine."[50]

Finally, the Eucharist is the messianic banquet. The messianic banquet is a figure of the joys of the messianic kingdom. The prophet Isaiah spoke of the Lord's preparing a banquet for those who are redeemed on Mt. Zion (25:6), and the monks of the Qumran community celebrated an anticipation of the messianic banquet. That the Eucharist is a banquet is evident from the fact that communion with the deity is implicit in the formulae of institution. Jesus' saying about not drinking again of the "fruit of the vine" until the Kingdom of God comes makes the identification explicit.

Luke's reconstruction brings his eschatological saying to the beginning of the institution account, which may well be its original position. It was relegated to the end of the liturgical formula recorded by Mark and Matthew because this was the only place where the cup was still mentioned. "Certainly the Eucharist stands, in the words of Benoit, in 'the eschatological present,' the

[48] *Op. cit.*, 64f.
[49] *Ibid.*, 65.
[50] Richardson, *op. cit.*, 371.

present which is a memorial of the past and a hope of the future, because in the Eucharist the Christian apprehends the enduring reality of the atoning death and the glorified body of Jesus. The Eucharist is therefore celebrated 'until He come,' and affirms the assured hope of the eschatological fulfillment of the salvation into which it integrates the Christian."[51]

THE ACTS OF THE APOSTLES

The coming of Jesus is the new definitive Exodus — this is the burden of the Gospels' message. The New Testament used the Exodus, the decisive divine act of the Old Testament period, to set forth its own meaning. It remained for St. Luke and the other later writings of the New Testament to apply this usage to the period of the Church. The Church itself is explained by the Exodus theology and other still more vivid usages of the Exodus theology are elaborated.

It is in this light that Professor Marsh considers the Acts of the Apostles in his study of New Testament theology. The pattern he discerns is one of grandeur. Professor Marsh writes: "The Gospels tell the story of the coming of the new Son or people of God in the person of Jesus Christ, and point their meaning by Exodus analogies. The book of Acts tells the story of the coming of the Son or people of God in the community of the Church, and points its meanings by Exodus and gospel analogies. The life of the new corporate son, like that of the new individual Son, bears the stamp of the Exodus pattern. If we may think of the cross and resurrection, which fulfilled the baptism for the individual son, as *the* baptism of the new corporate son (thus giving a basis for Paul's teaching on baptism as 'dying with Christ'), then the forty days of the tabernacling and teaching of the Lord are the Exodus imprint of the preparation in the wilderness, and the gift of the Spirit at Pentecost, with phenomena associated with the giving of the law on Sinai, is the enactment of the new law, not on tables of stone, but upon human hearts. The miracle of Pentecost was not the wind or the fire, or even the speaking with tongues; it was the fact that at last lips that had been dumb now for the first time proclaimed Jesus as both Lord and Christ. This was the basis for a plea for repentance and bap-

[51] McKenzie, *op. cit.*, 251.

tism (cf. Mark 1:15), and we read elsewhere that, like Jesus, the early Church preached the Kingdom (Acts 8:12, 14:22, 20:25, 28:23, 30)."[52]

By New Testament times the Feast of Pentecost had come to have historical significance as the commemoration of the giving of the Law. This fact considerably influenced Luke's description of the first Christian Pentecost. The sound of the wind recalls Sinai, as also does the appearance of fire. "Wind" and "Spirit" are closely related in Hebrew and Greek speech and thought, and wind and fire appear in the story of the Lord "passing by" when Elijah visited the mountain of the Law (2 Kings 15:11). The Spirit and the fire of judgment belong to John the Baptist's expectation of the future coming of the "stronger one" (Luke 3:16). The crowd of Pentecost pilgrims, drawn from all over the Dispersion, is a foreshadowing of the world-wide mission which was about to begin from Jerusalem. The Christian Pentecost is a picture of all the nations hearing the gospel, each in its own tongue, as the Law was believed to have been proclaimed by angels at Sinai to all the nations in their own languages.

First Epistle of St. Peter

Whether St. Peter wrote this book or not, it clearly has many characteristics in common with Mark's Gospel, and traditionally Peter and Mark are closely associated. Not surprisingly, then, the Exodus theme is pronounced. Speaking of the present condition of Christians in the Church, Peter tells his readers that before their conversion they were like straying sheep, but as Christians they are sheep that have returned to the true shepherd of their souls (2:25). This shepherd gave his life for the sheep. Like a paschal lamb without spot or blemish, Christ ransomed them from futility (1:19).

Peter is keenly aware of the intimate bond connecting Christian baptism with the Exodus. Those who have been baptized in Christ are the New People of God (2:9). Redeemed by the spotless Lamb from their old life of sin, they may now live according to their divine likeness and follow the Lamb of Holiness (1:15). "With girded loins (1 Pet. 1:13; cf. Exod. 12:11), they can set out for the desert where they can worship God (1 Pet. 2:5;

[52] *Op. cit.*, 764.

cf. Exod. 5:1-5; 7:16 and *passim*), and drink from the Rock, that
is Christ, whence flow streams of life-giving water (1 Pet. 2:4;
cf. Exod. 17:6). Baptism is for Christians a new Exodus which
separates them from the world of sin so that they may give
themselves to God's worship."[53]

BOOK OF REVELATION

The Exodus stands at the head of God's saving acts in history
and all later phases of salvation history explain themselves by
making use of this theme. Crossing the Jordan was a new Exodus; liberation from Babylonian captivity was a new Exodus.
Jesus presented himself as the definitive Exodus. The Christian
life in the time of the Church, between the Ascension and the
Parousia, is also presented in terms of the Exodus. It was inevitable then that the consummation of all things should be presented in Exodus terminology as well and that consequently it
should figure prominently in the book of Revelation.

For all its strange and puzzling imagery the Apocalypse uses
the fundamental theological themes of the New Testament.
"Revelation, by its emphasis upon what is to happen at and before the end of history, brings into sharp relief one essential fac-
tor in the whole range of thinking that begins with the life of
Jesus as reported in the Gospels. Jesus knew that his own life was
a 'fulfilment' of the story of the ancient people of God; he knew
that his own baptism was a fulfilment of the baptism of the old
people of God in the Red Sea, of their baptism in the Jordan
under Joshua; but he also knew that his baptism in Jordan was
also something that had to be fulfilled, and it is plain that he
saw the fulfilment in the cross and resurrection. It is equally plain
that neither he nor the Church saw even the cross and resurrection as the end 'absolutely'; still the people of God must await a
fulfilment; and Revelation underlines this."[54]

The work of deliverance accomplished by Jesus through his
triumph on the Cross has not yet worked out its full effects. "We
live during the intermediary period when the Spirit of God, given
by Christ, still struggles with Satan, the Spirit of evil. The work
of deliverance will be complete only at the end of time, when

---

[53] Giblet, *op. cit.*, 222f.
[54] Marsh, *op. cit.*, 766.

Satan and all hostile powers, including death, will be made powerless by God. The Apocalypse describes this final and complete victory in terms of the great theme of the Exodus."[55] It was the Lord who began the plan of salvation in the Exodus from Egypt and it is the Lord who will work out its ultimate consequences. The faithful have been saved by him "who art and who wast" (Apoc. 11:17; 16:5), and they will be saved by him "who is and who was and who is to come" (Apoc. 1:4; 4:8). This is an obvious allusion to the sacred Name I AM, once revealed to Moses. It is Yahweh, I AM, who will deliver his people.

God's enemies and those of his people will be struck with plagues which plainly resemble those released by Moses against Pharaoh and the Egyptians. The vision of the seven bowls contains many allusions to the Exodus plagues. When the second angel sounded the trumpet "a great mountain, burning with fire, was thrown into the sea; and a third of the sea became blood" (Apoc. 8:8). The first angel poured out his bowl "and foul and evil sores came upon the men who bore the mark of the beast and worshipped its image (Apoc. 16:2). This is reminiscent of the sixth Egyptian plague, the plague of boils (Exod. 19:8-12). When the second angel "poured out his bowl into the sea, it became like the blood of a dead man, and every living thing died that was in the sea" (Apoc. 16:3).

The Exodus tradition then seems to be one of the most fundamental in Scripture. All stages of redemptive history subsequent to this first event used the Exodus to explain its own meaning. If modern readers no longer feel completely at home with it, this is only because they have lost their Scriptural heritage to a large degree.

In a recent essay on typology, Professor Lampe notes that the ordinary reader of a century ago seems to have taken a large measure of typology in his stride. Most of the typology he met with was standard and traditional. But, more important, that reader shared a common cultural tradition with the New Testament writers. This imaginary reader of a hundred years ago "was still, like the men of the first century, the heir of Biblical and Hebraic culture. The world of the Hebrew Scriptures was still familiar to him, and it was natural for him to follow the early Christian interpreters in expressing his experience of redemption

---

[55] Giblet, *op. cit.*, 228.

in Christ in thought-forms derived from the exodus from Egyptian bondage and entrance into the Promised Land, or to see the escape of the Israelites as a picture, bearing some real though undefined relation to what is portrayed, of man's deliverance from the devil's tyranny through the saving work of Christ."[56]

As we shall see in the next part of this study, Christians found one part of the Exodus tradition, that of the Wilderness, particularly applicable to their condition during the interim period of the Church. This earthly life of ours corresponds to Israel's pilgrimage through the desert. And, as T. F. Glasson points out in his *Moses in the Fourth Gospel*, when Christians become thoroughly imbued with the Bible's teaching, this correspondence comes home to them and becomes part of their everyday thought and speech. In particular, Negro spirituals teach us what it means to "Cross the Jordan." "The earthly life with its travail and burdensome wanderings is at length to be exchanged for the promised land of Canaan on the other side of the river of death, the River Jordan. . . . This familiar usage is not merely an apt fragment of metaphorical language; it is based upon a long Christian tradition which reaches back to the New Testament itself and which has been worked out in a whole series of comparisons and correspondences. All the main events of Israel's story, from the bondage in Egypt to the conquests of Joshua, found their counterpart in Christian experience."[57]

[56] *Op. cit.*, 11.
[57] *Op. cit.*, 9.

Part Two

THE WILDERNESS
OLD TESTAMENT

The Lord's first great saving act, the Exodus, cast its shadow over all future divine, saving acts. But the Exodus is itself a complex of events. It includes the calling of Moses, the contest with Pharaoh, the crossing of the Red Sea, the whole wilderness period (which itself includes a great many incidents), and, finally, the entrance into the Promised Land. Basic to all of these, no doubt, is the idea of divine deliverance. But each phase of the Exodus has its own message, bringing some aspect of this divine deliverance to the fore and presenting it in a new, more revealing light. And paradoxically, it is the wilderness or desert period that has one of the most important lessons to teach us.

Thus, paradoxically again, the desert or wilderness is one of the most fertile geographical concepts in Scripture. This is due primarily to the forty years spent in the desert between the Exodus and the conquest, and to the striking use that St. Mark makes of the Wilderness theme in his Gospel. Just how basic the Wilderness theme is to St. Mark's Gospel has been impressively demonstrated by Ulrich W. Mauser in his recent work *Christ in the Wilderness*.[1]

God chose the Israelites and made them his special people. But the Chosen People found that their great privilege, their special grace, meant their being led out into the desert, into the wilderness. And life in the wilderness proved to be a life of the greatest hardship and danger. Life was uncertain; even food and water were lacking. Unless God sustained them from day to day, they would perish.

Thus the Israelites found the place of God's special grace a

[1] *Passim.*

53

place of trial and temptation, and, because their faith was not perfect, they made it a place of murmuring and rebellion. They longed for the soft life and tasty dishes they had enjoyed in Egypt; they demanded to be led into the land of the Lord's rest before the hour willed by the Lord. They found that the grace that God had given them was not irrevocable. Alas, for many of them the place of God's special grace became a place of death and destruction. This very basic pattern of events and circumstances left its imprint on all future stages of God's plan of salvation.

The word used most frequently in the Old Testament to denote desert or wilderness (*midbar*) is derived from a root whose original meaning was "to drive." The *midbar* is the place where the cattle are driven. The word does not necessarily convey the meaning of sand desert with absolutely no vegetation; rather it means sparsely inhabited, barren plains which, however, provide enough pasturage for herds. This is "'steppe, prairie land,' where there is a short-lived growth of grass after the winter rains, but where these rains are generally not in sufficient quantity for raising farm crops. Most of the land to the south and east of Palestine is a desert in this sense."[2]

This is "a land not sown," (Jer. 2:2). But, at least in the spring, there are green fields here, where sheep can be pastured and cisterns dug to hold the winter rain. But without rain, it is a "desert in which there is no man, a waste and a desolate land" (Job 38:26-27). Wild asses, jackals, ostriches, owls, and poisonous snakes inhabit its untilled ranges, where thorns and briers thrive.

DANGER AND DIVINE HELP

On the shores of the Sea of Reeds the fugitive slaves saw Pharaoh and his chariots and his horsemen overwhelmed by the waters. Miriam sang: "Sing to the Lord, for he has triumphed gloriously; the horse and his rider he has thrown into the sea" (Exod. 15:19-21). Then the fugitives turned their backs on Egypt and made their way into the wilderness of Sinai. The march through the desert which follows, the forty years in the wilderness, is a time characterized by danger and divine help. "The wilderness is the place that threatens the very existence of Yah-

[2] Van den Born – Hartman, *Encyclopedic Dictionary of the Bible*, 551.

weh's chosen people, but it is also the stage which brightly il-
lumines God's power and readiness to dispel the threat."[3]

As soon as they moved into the wastes of the Sinai Peninsula,
the fugitives found themselves threatened with disaster. It was
not because of any daring-do on their or Moses' part that they
had set out on this undertaking. It was in obedience to the Lord's
commandment as spoken through Moses. Now it seems that obedience to this command can only lead to annihilation. "The journey was difficult. Freedom in the desert was, to many of the
pilgrims, a poor substitute for slavery in Egypt. Water was scarce;
there was no food; existence was precarious. It is a tribute to the
realism of the narrators that, instead of idealizing the past, they
present life as it surely must have been. It was a time of murmuring, discontent, internal strife, rebellion against Moses, and,
above all, lack of faith. Despite all that had happened, the people cried out: 'Is Yahweh among us or not?' (Exod. 17:7)."[4]

But the march through the desert is equally the time of the
Lord's continuous help. Yahweh's words to the pilgrims on the
eve of the theophany at Sinai are the most authentic commentary
to all events during the wilderness wanderings: "You have seen
what I did to the Egyptians, and how I bore you on eagles' wings
and brought you to myself" (Exod. 19:4). Whenever the Hebrews
thirst, water is given; whenever they hunger, food is provided.
But they are instructed to gather only enough manna for their
"daily bread." They are not permitted to live in security lest they
forget their utter dependence on God.

At length the pilgrims reach the oasis of Sinai. There they experience divine interventions which are once for all decisive and
normative for their religious life. On the basis of his mighty deeds
on their behalf, the Lord grants the fugitives a covenant and the
Law, the terms of the covenant. These acts are the visible manifestation of the Lord's earlier election of this group to be his
chosen people, and they form the disparate group into a people,
Israel.

THE MOLTEN CALF

But even so, the remainder of Israel's time in the desert was a
time of rebellion. Since the flight from Egypt was undertaken at

[3] Mauser, *op. cit.*, 21.
[4] B. Anderson, *Understanding the Old Testament*, 50.

the Lord's command, the fact that the people lose courage is not
interpreted as a breakdown of noble decision, but as a rebellion
against God. Repeated small acts of rebellion lead to a more
serious instance. After the giving of the covenant, Moses ascends
the Mount with Joshua to receive the stone tablets, and remains
forty days to receive further commands. "When the people saw
that Moses delayed to come down from the mountain, the people
gathered themselves together to Aaron, and said to him, 'Up,
make us gods, who shall go before us; as for this Moses, the man
who brought us up out of the land of Egypt, we do not know
what has become of him. . . . So all the people took off the rings
of gold which were in their ears, and brought them to Aaron.
And he received the gold at their hand, and fashioned it with a
graving tool, and made a molten calf; and they said, 'These are
your gods, O Israel, who brought you up out of the land of
Egypt!'" (Exod. 32:1, 3-4).

This may well represent some retrojection, or as Mauser puts
it with great caution: "The inexplicable and ineradicable bias to
idolatry which assumes the shape of the worship of images when
Israel is surrounded by Canaanite culture is already operative
in the desert at the time of the establishment of the covenant."[5]

After the molten calf is set up, Aaron builds an altar before it
and proclaims: "Tomorrow shall be a feast of the Lord" (v. 5).
It does not seem that there was any overt intention of repudiating
Yahweh. "Two or three centuries later, *bull images* again emerge
in the history of Israel. Among the measures taken by Jeroboam I
for the consolidation of his new kingdom was one which was
primarily designed to secure its independence of the rival kingdom of the South in the all-important matter of public worship.
With this end in view, perhaps also with the subsidiary purpose
of reconciling the priesthood of the local sanctuaries to the new
order of things, Jeroboam set up two golden 'calves,' one at Bethel
and the other at Dan, the two most important sanctuaries, geo-
graphically and historically, in his realm (1 Kings 12:26-33)."[6]

It is generally agreed that it was Jeroboam's intention that the
bulls should be looked upon as symbols of Yahweh, but it is also
possible that they were pedestals on which Yahweh's image
stood. That the bull became popularly treated as an image can

[5] Mauser, *op. cit.*, 30.
[6] J. Hastings, *Dictionary of the Bible*, 119.

scarcely be doubted. The bull or calf, the central image of Canaanite worship of fertility, is the representation of the blessings of nature in a land of agriculture. To worship of fertility deities belong public feasting and sexual orgies. And the text of Exodus says that after offering burnt offerings before the molten calf the Israelites "sat down to eat and drink, and rose up to play" (32:6). "Plainly," says Mauser, "the Israelites are tired of the life in the desert; they long for plentiful food and enjoyment. A land of rich fertility had been promised them, it is true, but the time is not yet ripe for them to enter it. Only God himself can rightfully bring their wanderings to an end, as he alone had led them out into the wilderness. Israel makes an attempt to shorten the time of waiting, seeking to escape the desert before God allows them to do so" (p. 31).

If at this point the Exodus experience has possibly reached forward to embrace something of the later Canaan experience, it leaves its imprint on Israel's earlier history as well. The patriarchs are not only individuals but are also made to embody Israel's characteristics and experience. And surely one of the strongest notes in the patriarchs' stories is that they were wanderers, dependent upon the Lord for their daily sustenance. "The patriarchs were wanderers toward a goal that Yahweh had set before them. Their history was a nomadic movement from promise toward fulfillment, not an aimless quest for pastureland for their flocks. Yet it was not easy for them to live by the promise, for again and again they found themselves in situations that made the promise seem incredible. At such times their trust in Yahweh was put to a severe test, and they were moved to the verge of despair. In episode after episode the Yahwist builds up a sense of dramatic suspense, only to resolve it by showing how Yahweh intervened at the critical moment, just when everything seemed lost, and renewed the promise."[7]

TEMPTATION IN THE WILDERNESS

The wilderness period was a time when the Lord "tempted" Israel and when Israel "tempted" the Lord. The words "tempt" and "temptation" are, in the Old Testament, nearly always translations of various forms of a root (*nissah*) which is properly rendered

[7] B. Anderson, *op. cit.*, 176.

"prove" or "test." The idea is to test or prove a person, to see whether he will act in a particular way, or whether the character he bears is well established. God thus proves a person, or puts him to the test, to see if his fidelity or affection is sincere. And men test or prove the Lord when they act as if doubting whether his promise is true or whether he is faithful to his revealed character.[8]

Fleeing Israel left the shores of the Red Sea and passed into the wilderness of Shur. They went three days without water and when they came to Marah they found the water bitter and could not drink it. The people murmur against Moses and he cried to the Lord. After the water is made sweet at the Lord's direction, we read in the book of Exodus that "there the Lord made for them a statute and an ordinance and there he proved them, saying, 'If you will diligently hearken to the voice of the Lord your God . . . I will put none of the diseases upon you which I put upon the Egyptians'" (Exod. 15:25-26). Probably a proving is mentioned in this connection because of the similarity between Marah and Massah (Exod. 17:1-7).

When the Israelites came to the wilderness of Sin they again murmured against Moses because there was no food. The Lord told Moses: "Behold, I will rain bread from heaven for you; and the people shall go out and gather a day's portion every day, that I may prove them, whether they will walk in my law or not" (Exod. 16:4). Then Israel moved on from the Wilderness of Sin and camped at Rephidim and the people murmured against Moses because there was no water. And Moses said: "Why do you find fault with me? Why do you put the Lord to the proof?" (Exod. 17:2). After Moses produced water by striking the rock at the Lord's direction, he called the name of the place Massah (Proof) and Meribah (Contention), because of the fault-finding of the children of Israel, and because they put the Lord to the proof by saying, 'Is the Lord among us or not?'" (Exod. 17:7).

The people did not prove equal to the test given them by the Lord, and "their fault lay in 'tempting God' in their turn. The same words, the verb *nasah* and the noun *massah*, express the two temptations and place them in the same episodes. At the waters of Mara, Yahweh tempts His people; at the waters of Massah, it

[8] Cf. Hastings, 968.

is the people which tempts Yahweh. The murmurings and the revolt of the people of the desert are just so many temptations of God."[9]

REMEMBER THE WILDERNESS

The temptation theme is especially strong in Deuteronomy. In its present form, the whole book of Deuteronomy purports to be a sermon given by Moses to Israel in Moab, just before the people crossed over the Jordan River to take possession of the Promised Land. This is a crucial moment and Moses exhorts them to remember the Lord's saving acts in the Exodus and the wilderness and to hold firm to their covenant pledge during the days to come. Without a doubt the Exodus experience has reached forward here to incorporate the sad results of Israel's encounter with the Canaanite nature cult.

It is the wilderness period especially that becomes the text for Moses' sermon. The period in the desert must never be forgotten. This time established a lesson which the nation must remember in order to attain the fruition of the promise. Again and again the people are warned — *remember*! They must remember the unprecedented and miraculous help of Yahweh during the Exodus and in the wilderness. They must remember the stubborn rebellion of an intractable people. Moses admonishes the people: "You shall remember all the way which the Lord your God has led you these forty years in the wilderness, that he might humble you, testing you to know what was in your heart, whether you would keep his commandments, or not" (Deut. 8:2). The Lord tested the people and because they were found wanting, they tempted him in turn.

Yahweh tested, disciplined, humbled Israel to burn into her heart the secret of her election. He tested her so that she might find out what was in her heart. Mauser writes: "Interpreted like this the idea of testing would well fit the similar one of humbling, ideas which are tied together in 8:2 and 16. The purpose of the test is Israel's self-recognition which consists in humility. Humility, and not pride, is the proper response to Yahweh's election, as Israel is not chosen because she is bigger (Deut. 7:7) or better (Deut. 9:4) than other peoples. More than that, self-recognition in the light of election even means the recognition of sinfulness

[9] J Guillet, *Themes of the Bible*, 8f.

(9:7). For that reason Deuteronomy repeated the story of the golden calf in Exod. 32" (p. 35).

In speaking of the wilderness period, the Pentateuch stresses the dangers which are inseparable from life in the desolate, barren wastes. Moses admonishes the people in his farewell discourse: "Take heed lest you forget the Lord your God . . . who led you through the great and terrible wilderness, with its fiery serpents and scorpions and thirsty ground where there was no water" (Deut. 8:11, 15). This passage sums up the underlying concept in all wilderness stories in the Pentateuch. The wilderness is the foil showing off the greatness of God's actions on the one hand and the rebellion of the people on the other. So, Moses continues, this same Lord God "brought you water out of the flinty rock, fed you in the wilderness with manna which your fathers did not know, that he might humble you and test you, to do you good in the end" (Deut. 8:16).

The Psalms often praise God for his mighty deeds in behalf of his people but rarely do they cite examples from the period of desert wandering. In the Psalms the element of Israel's rebellion in the desert occupies a central position. In Psalm 78 the Lord's acts of mercy provide the background against which the sins of the people stand out. The Lord acted again and again to save his people, "yet they sinned still more against him, rebelling against the Most High in the desert. . . . How often they rebelled against him in the wilderness and grieved him in the desert!" (Ps. 78:17, 40).

In the course of time Israel borrowed imagery from Near Eastern mythology, especially creation stories, and we begin to find the wilderness regarded as one of the powers of chaos defeated by Yahweh when he intervenes to save his people. Just as Yahweh crushed the head of the Dragon when Israel passed through the Sea of Reeds, so he subdues the wild, chaotic powers of the wilderness, turns the desert into verdant pastures, as he guides and sustains his people in the wilderness. Thus we read in Psalm 68: "O God, when thou didst go forth before thy people, when thou didst march through the wilderness, the earth quaked, the heavens poured down rain, at the presence of God. . . . Rain in abundance, O God, thou didst shed abroad; thou didst restore thy heritage as it languished" (Ps. 68:7-9).

RETURN TO THE WILDERNESS

With the prophets a new element enters the Wilderness concept: the expectation of a new time which Israel will have to spend in the wilderness. Hosea's experience with Gomer pictures Yahweh's experience with Israel, fallen away to the worship of the Canaanite Baals to insure the fertility of the land. Israel says: "I will go after my lovers, who give me my bread and my water, my wool and my flax, my oil and my drink" (2:5). If Israel will not *return* to Yahweh she will have to *return* to the desert. "They shall return to the land of Egypt, and Assyria shall be their king, because they have refused to return to me" (11:5). "Return" (*shub*) is a word that occurs frequently in Hosea and it underlies the New Testament concept of repentance.

Israel's return to the desert comes as a result of God's wrath and judgment. Israel's children should plead with her, "lest I strip her naked and make her as in the day she was born, and make her like a wilderness, and set her like a parched land, and slay her with thirst" (2:3). Yet the return to the desert condition is the renewal of hope. "I will allure her, and bring her into the wilderness, and speak tenderly to her. . . . And there she shall answer as in the days of her youth" (2:14-15). By returning to the desert Israel can return to the original relationship with Yahweh, to the genuine status of sonship to God. Thus the idea that a return to God is a return to the wilderness becomes a part of Old Testament thought.

Unfortunately, of course, Israel did not return to the Lord and therefore had to return to the wilderness. But in the course of time it became Second Isaiah's happy commission to proclaim a New Exodus. "In the wilderness prepare the way of the Lord, make straight in the desert a highway for our God. Every valley shall be lifted up, and every mountain and hill be made low; the uneven ground shall become level, and the rough places a plain" (Is. 40:3-4). The exodus out of the dispersion back to Palestine will again be a passage through the wilderness. As the Lord slew the Dragon of Chaos in the first Exodus, so now every chaotic aspect of the wilderness, everything troublesome for the journey of the redeemed will be transformed into a condition insuring easy passage.

Under God's wrath and judgment the good land is turned into

a state of chaos again. Conversely, when the Lord acts to save, the wilderness is turned to verdant pastures. The Lord manifested his protecting and guiding presence to the Israelites in the wilderness of Sinai by the pillar of fire, identified with the Spirit of the Lord already in ancient interpretation (Is. 63:11). So in the New Exodus there will be a new outpouring of the Spirit which will transform the desert wastes to verdant pastures. "For I will pour water on the thirsty land, and streams on the dry ground; I will pour my Spirit upon your descendants, and my blessing on your offspring. They shall spring up like grass amid waters, like willows by flowing streams" (Is. 44:3-4).

As the message of the Dead Sea Scrolls has become clearer, it has become evident that, as the time of realization drew near, there were those in Judaism who took Second Isaiah's prophecy with all seriousness. Father Milik writes that the Essenes "interpreted Is. 40:3, 'The voice of one crying: in the wilderness prepare ye the way of the Lord, make straight in the desert a highway for our God' (cf. IQ S VIII 15f; IX 19ff.), as commanding a separation from wicked men, and a life in the desert studying and practising the Law according to its true meaning which had been revealed to them." [10] And Kurt Schubert writes that the Essenes "fled into the desert not only to be safe from the Syrian intervention troops but also because they regarded the desert as the place of salvation where the divine redemption would first reveal itself. Isaiah 40:3 may well have brought about such an attitude. In any case the Manual of Discipline of Qumran (8:12-14) says, 'when they join themselves together into a community in Israel in conformity with these regulations they must separate themselves from the dwelling place of sinners and go to the wilderness to prepare there the way of the Lord, as it is written, "In the wilderness prepare the way of the Lord, make straight in the desert a highway for our God."' Also in the War Scroll (1:2) the community itself is called a 'desert emigration.'"

The Qumran Essenes seem to be one of the outgrowths of the Hasidim of the Maccabean period. This pietist movement, whose members were drawn from priesthood and laity, combined fierce nationalism with religious, messianic fervor. This resistance group lent its support to the Maccabeans during the persecution of Antiochus Epiphanes. But soon the more religious group within

---

[10] *Ten Years of Discovery in the Wilderness of Judaea*, 116.

the general Hasidic movement broke with the Maccabees. The Hasmonaeans took over the high priesthood even though they could not claim any descent from Aaron and this the Essenes-to-be could not accept. They abandoned Jerusalem for exile at Qumran.

And their choice of this spot does not seem to have been dictated solely either by chance or the physical features of the spot. They did not choose a virgin site. There are clear traces of a previous occupation, dating from the eighth and seventh centuries. From the detailed list of place names in Joshua 15, it is even possible to recover the Israelite names of these settlements. And Mauser concludes: "The site of Qumran has been identified with what is called the City of Salt in Josh. 15:61. Joshua lists six villages which together form the district of the wilderness (*midbar*) indicating that the wilderness condition was regarded as so constitutive for the region that it could provide the name for a province at the time when the list of Judaean places in Josh. 15 was composed" (p. 58). This circumstance may well have influenced the choice of this site for the monastery of Qumran and also the sojourn of John the Baptist in the desert.

The Qumran community looked upon itself as the New Israel. The members of the community have entered a new covenant, while Israel as a whole has gone astray. Leaving the world and entering the community is a return (*shub*), a turning from sin and a turning to God, a repentance. The Essenes believed that they had been called to repeat the experience of their forefathers who had lived forty years in the desert, while overcoming the trials through which that generation had failed to come successfully. When they first established themselves in the Wilderness of Judea, they predicted that their stay would last for forty years, showing that they conceived this time as parallel to their forefathers' desert sojourn. The community is subdivided into tribes, thousands, and the like, according to the pattern which the Pentateuch ascribes to the wilderness period. "Being conscious of living in the last days before the arrival of the Messiah, the community had to prepare the way where, according to prophetic announcements, it had to be prepared — in the desert. This shows the great strength of the wilderness concept and its combination with the picture of eschatology."[11]

[11] Mauser, *op. cit.*, 61.

NEW TESTAMENT

How meaningful, then, is the fact that all three Synoptics proclaim at the head of their Gospels the fulfillment of Isaiah's prophecy in Jesus' coming. "The beginning of the gospel of Jesus Christ, the Son of God," St. Mark writes in his first verse, and immediately he ties Jesus' coming to Isaiah's great prophecy and the Wilderness tradition as a whole. The first thirteen verses of St. Mark, which relate the activity of John the Baptist, the baptism of Jesus, and the temptation, are a single unit. The three incidents are tied together by the common wilderness locale. Only the Jordan is mentioned in connection with Jesus' baptism, but against the background of the book of Joshua and the Qumran community, it is easy to see that the lower reaches of the Jordan form part of the "wilderness district." In addition, it has been observed that Mark often strings together traditions by the use of key-words. In this instance it is the word "Spirit" that appears in all three sections.

Eschatological Prophet

St. Mark immediately connected Jesus' coming to Isaiah's prophecy of a second Exodus. Mark 1:2 begins: "As it is written in Isaiah the prophet." But St. Mark prefixes Isaiah's prophecy with the evocative line: "Behold, I send my messenger before me" (v. 2). On Sinai the Lord assured Moses: "Behold, I send an angel before you to guard you on the way and to bring you to the place which I have prepared" (Exod. 23:20).

This line was taken up again in postexilic times by the prophet Malachi. When the people were saying that Yahweh is indifferent to what is right and that he is not a God of justice, the prophet Malachi proclaimed that they would learn the truth when he came for judgment and appeared like a refiner's fire: "Behold, I send my messenger to prepare the way before me, and the Lord whom you seek will suddenly come to his temple" (3:1). Later in the same book Elijah is identified with this messenger: "Behold, I will send you Elijah the prophet before the great and terrible day of the Lord comes. And he will turn the hearts of fathers to their children and the hearts of children to their fathers, lest I come and smite the land with a curse" (Mal. 4:5-6).

The messenger, the one crying in the wilderness, prepares the

way of the Lord, who is announced in the wilderness and
whose coming will be through the wilderness. All the remainder
of Mark's prologue (1:1-13) is a comment on this prophecy. In
both its aspects this prophecy is anchored in the Wilderness tradition. Thus our attention is concentrated on three factors: the
Messenger, the Lord, and the Wilderness.

And it is clear that in Mark the wilderness is not mentioned
in order to give geographical fixture to the record but to fix Jesus
in the Wilderness tradition. Mark makes no attempt to designate
a precise location. D. E. Nineham writes in the Pelican Commentary: "St. Mark has no interest in locating the wilderness or help-
ing his readers to do so; it is simply the wilderness of the
prophecy."[12] Matthew and Luke were not satisfied with this
indefiniteness and give more precise references to locality ("wilderness of Judea," "region about the Jordan"). Mark's prime con-
cern is the Wilderness theology as such.

After the prophecy Mark presents the Herald. "John the baptizer appeared in the wilderness" (Mark 1:4). "In the wilderness"
appears also in the prophecy of the second Exodus which appears
at the beginning of Second Isaiah: "In the wilderness prepare
the way of the Lord" (Is. 40:3). It is the key-phrase linking John
with the prophecy and the Wilderness theology. John's food and
clothing link him with Elijah.

The book of Kings relates that King Ahaziah of Israel, successor
of Ahab and Jezebel, fell through the lattice of his upper chamber
in Samaria, and lay sick. He sent messengers to inquire at a
Canaanite shrine whether he would recover. On their way to the
shrine the messengers were met by Elijah, who told them to return to their master and tell him that he was to die for his act
of infidelity. Ahaziah asked: "'What kind of man was he who
came to meet you and told you these things?' They answered
him, 'He wore a garment of haircloth, with a girdle of leather
about his loins.' And he said, 'It is Elijah the Tishbite'" (2 Kings
1:7-8).

BAPTISM OF REPENTANCE

It is John's ministry to prepare the way of the Lord by preaching the baptism of repentance. The fact that the call to repentance

---

[12] D. E. Nineham, *Gospel of St. Mark,* 57.

and the baptism take place "in the wilderness" gives us the clue to Mark's understanding. The decisive event in the history of salvation has now begun to unfold itself. The expectation of a new wilderness period heralding the eschatological consummation is now at hand. Repentance, in the sense of a return to the desert (*shub*) in preparation for a return to the Lord, is now proclaimed. What the Qumran community was awaiting is now at hand. The march into the desert is the repentance to which John calls.

Proselytes to Judaism at that time were baptized because it was felt that the convert should undergo the same experience that Israel as a people had once undergone in passing through the Red Sea. "By John's baptism of repentance for the forgiveness of sins in the setting that Mark gives it by association with Malachi, Isaiah and Elijah, we are to understand that it was related in imagery to the crossing of the Red Sea under Moses (the baptism of the 'old Israel,' cf. 1 Cor. 10:1, 2), and that John was calling his people to repent of their past, to confess their sins, to be baptized, i.e., enter the new Israel, because he was profoundly convinced that there was about to come among them one who would give the reality of which his (John's) baptism was still only a symbol."[13]

Israel must repent; she must return to the desert because she has not returned to the Lord. The desert is the place of judgment and purification. Israel can re-establish her position as God's beloved people only by surrendering her rebellious ways. The return to the wilderness means the acknowledgment and repudiation of her disobedient past and a determination to make a fresh start.

After the messenger who prepares the way, St. Mark's prologue introduces the Lord who will follow, whose way is being prepared (1:9-11). There is an anonymous allusion to the Lord already in v. 8, a linking verse: "I have baptized you with water, but he will baptize you with the Holy Spirit." Matthew and Luke say that the mightier one will baptize "with the Holy Spirit and with fire." This is in line with their emphasis on the Messiah as Judge. They both add the picture of the Messiah clearing his threshing floor with his winnowing fork (Matthew 3:12; Luke 3:17). Fire is an established symbol of judgment.

[13] J. Marsh, "Theology of the New Testament," in *Peake's Commentary on the Bible*, 759.

The original reference may have been to wind and fire, both being used as symbols of judgment (*pneuma*, the "spirit" of v. 8, and its Hebrew and Aramaic equivalents can mean both wind and spirit). In which case "Holy" (*hagio*) would then be a Christian interpretative addition. This gives a highly plausible connection with the other Synoptics — the wind carrying away the chaff. "But, as there is evidence that a general bestowal of the Spirit was expected as a feature of the last days (see esp. Joel 2:28f; also Is. 32:15; 44:3; Ezek. 36:25-27; 37:14; 39:29), and also some evidence, though not much, that the Messiah was expected, not only to be equipped with the Spirit, but actually himself to bestow the Spirit (Test. Levi 18:11), it seems more probable that the original saying of John did contain a reference to the bestowal of the Spirit. If the Mt./Lk. form is original, then the meaning would be that the coming one would bring the eschatological judgment."[14]

In any case there is a striking contrast between Jesus the giver of life (Mark 1:8) and Jesus the humble penitent (Mark 1:9) receiving baptism at John's hands. Later in his life when the sons of Zebedee asked to sit at his right and left hand, Jesus asked them: "Are you able to drink the cup that I drink, or to be baptized with the baptism with which I am baptized?" (Mark 10:38). Both cup and baptism are recognized symbols of God's wrath and judgment. Jesus' baptism is his becoming subject to God's judgment. Jesus' mission is one of enduring God's judgment for the sake of others, culminating in his crucifixion. What is begun in his baptism will be continued throughout his ministry and will be resolved in his death.

Set in the overall Wilderness theology, Jesus' baptism at John's hands is of the greatest significance. "John's appearance in the wilderness, his call to repentance and his baptism imply the conviction that the time has come when God will execute this last and all-decisive judgment in which a new Israel will emerge. Jesus fully acknowledges this conviction (Mark 11:30). He is himself willing to shoulder the burden of this judgment and bear it in his whole mission."[15]

[14] C. E. B. Cranfield, *Gospel according to Saint Mark*, 50.
[15] Mauser, *op. cit.*, 92.

The One and the Many

When John the baptizer appeared in the wilderness, St. Mark relates that "all the country of Judea and all the people of Jerusalem" went out to him and were baptized in the Jordan (1:5). Later he relates that "Jesus came from Nazareth of Galilee and was baptized in the Jordan (Mark 1:9). Judea and Jerusalem represent the holy province and the sacred capital; Galilee the suspect, half-heathen north. The many come out from Judea and Jerusalem and show themselves the very opposite of newborn creatures. One comes out from Galilee, the one true penitent, the beloved Son of God, as the voice from heaven proclaims.

But this is more than a mere individual. Designating Jesus as the "beloved Son," the voice from heaven identifies him with the Suffering Servant of Second Isaiah and in the course of the Servant poems the Servant concept shifts from a corporate to an individual meaning. The Son of Man title which Jesus was to use so extensively during his ministry also has a strong corporate background in the book of Daniel. And both concepts leave room for the idea of victory through suffering. God's "pleasure" in Jesus indicates that the life of the new "Son" or "people" of God would, like that of the Servant of Isaiah, attain its victorious denouement through suffering and death.

Baptized by John, Jesus indicated his self-identification with his own people and his repentance with and for them. "When he came out of the water (in the imagery of the Mosaic Exodus, when he came to the place where a new relationship with and service of God could be initiated), he heard a voice from heaven which said: 'Thou art my beloved son; with thee I am well pleased.' In the Exodus imagery context this means that in Jesus God sees the new beginning of the life of his people (cf. Hos. 11:1, 'When Israel was a child I loved him, and out of Egypt I called my son.'"[16] Naturally we think also of Matthew's application of Hosea's verse to the flight into Egypt: "This was to fulfil what the Lord had spoken by the prophet, 'Out of Egypt have I called my son'" (Matthew 2:15).

In the wilderness Israel is first designated to be the son of Yahweh, and in the event of Israel's return to the desert her sonship will be renewed. In Jesus the old prophecy is fulfilled. Israel

---

[16] J. Marsh, *op. cit.*, 759.

is, so to speak, concentrated in the person of Jesus. "In re-crossing Egypt, the Jordan, or the desert, Jesus is doing something quite different from pious pilgrimages over the footprints left by His people. He is remaking, on His own account, the people's spiritual journey. Triumphing over the trial in the desert, He reveals Himself to be, alone, the faithful people, the authentic Israel, the Son of God." [17]

Jesus is, from the beginning of the Gospel, more than a mere individual; he is the New People of God, its life and its reality. "What the baptism of the many did not bring about is achieved in the true penitence of the man from Galilee. Thus, his exodus into the wilderness to John is shown to be the only valid exodus. All others have only physically gone out to Jordan — they returned to their Judean homes basically unrepentant. Only Jesus fully realized what it meant to go out into the wilderness: It meant the determination to live under the judgment of God." [18]

As the baptized Jesus comes up out of the water, the Spirit comes down upon him like a dove. Jewish associations between dove and spirit were of long standing and the outpouring of the Spirit to come with the New Exodus of the last days is a frequent element in the prophetic and later writings.

JESUS IN THE DESERT

St. Mark's account of the temptation of Jesus has a number of remarkable features. He writes that after the baptism, "the Spirit immediately drove Jesus out into the wilderness. And he was in the wilderness forty days, tempted by Satan; and he was with the wild beasts; and the angels ministered to him" (Mark 1:12-13). It is remarkably succinct. No description of the actual temptation is given nor is a final victory indicated. The statement that Jesus was "with the wild beasts" is unusual. But everything is wonderfully adapted to the Wilderness theology. Mark's account was not meant to be primarily a temptation story at all, as in the other Synoptics, but a description of Jesus' sojourn in the Wilderness. Thus a single theme, the Wilderness, is seen to run through the incidents of Mark's prologue: Jesus, announced and baptized in the desert, continues there for forty days.

[17] Guillet, *op. cit.*, 15f.
[18] Mauser, *op. cit.*, 96.

In Mark the baptism and temptation scenes are closely connected. The baptism scene has no proper conclusion and the same Spirit that descends upon Jesus "drives" him further into the wilderness. Jesus' expulsion into the desert is the necessary outcome of his baptism. The repentance of the one true penitent, the Son of God, the New Israel, is not complete with his baptism. By this further plunge into the desert St. Mark has an opportunity to indicate what it means to be in the wilderness, to be repentant. It means to be tempted by Satan and to be ministered to by the angels. Closing the prologue to St. Mark's Gospel, the verses are at the same time an apt culmination of the Wilderness theology, the prologue's unifying theme.

All the details of the passage serve the main Wilderness theme. As Israel the Son of old was led into the desert by a pillar of fire to be tempted, so Jesus the New Son is driven into the wilderness by the Spirit to be tempted by Satan. Jesus is forty days in the wilderness as Moses was on Mount Sinai for forty days, and as Elijah journeyed through the desert forty days and forty nights to the mount of God, sustained by "a cake baked on hot stones and a jar of water" supplied by an angel of the Lord (1 Kings 19:7). Both Moses and Elijah remain men of the wilderness to the last. Jesus does not leave the wilderness behind after these forty days. The forty days concentrate into one focal period the essence of the ministry of Moses, Elijah and Jesus, and define it in terms of the Wilderness theology.

The wilderness was the place of trial for the first Israel and so it was for the New Israel as well. In the desert of Sinai, however, Yahweh himself tempted his people with a view toward purifying and strengthening them. Now Satan, the head of all powers hostile to God, tempts the New Israel to undo the work that God is doing through him. In the wilderness of Sinai, Israel led a precarious existence, threatened continually by enemies and the harsh conditions of the terrain. Their survival hung in the balance from day to day. They were dependent upon the Lord for their *daily* bread. But by the same token, these were forty years of almost miraculous existence under the Lord's direct guidance. So now, in the wilderness the New Israel is with the beasts and the angels minister to him. On Sinai the Lord assured Moses: "Behold, I send an angel before you to guard you on the way and to bring you to the place which I have prepared" (Exod.

23:20). In his flight from Jezebel, Elijah was sustained by the bread and water supplied by an angel of the Lord. Here many angels minister to the new Son of God.

SATAN DETHRONED

It is significant that Mark does not report a victory over Satan. This is because he wished to emphasize the fact that the clash with Satan continues throughout the remainder of Jesus' ministry. For the same reason Mark did not have to indicate the content of the temptation. This is also shown by Jesus' ministry as a whole.

Later in his Gospel, St. Mark records Jesus as saying: "The Son of Man came not to be served but to serve and to give his life as a ransom for many" (Mark 10:45). And Jesus asked the sons of Zebedee: "Are you able to drink the cup that I drink, or to be baptized with the baptism with which I am baptized?" (Mark 10:38). St. Luke indicates the continuing struggle with Satan in a more explicit way, writing that "when the devil had ended every temptation, he departed from him until an opportune time" (4:13). "Until His hour has come," writes Father Guillet, "Jesus has not truly completed His Exodus. This hour is called by Jesus Himself His Baptism, the hour of the chalice which He must drink. Like St. Paul, Jesus interprets His Passion in a vocabulary which will later become that of the two great Christian sacraments, but which also links up with that of the Exodus. These verbal connections are the sign of profound contacts. Between the way in which Jesus accomplishes the Exodus of His people, and the way in which He establishes His sacraments, there is a kind of symmetry. Every year, the Hebrew people relived its Exodus in its liturgy. Jesus relived it, first in His heart, then, in His flesh and in His blood. This act definitively fulfilled and made forever vain the entire liturgy of Israel, which was directed toward a memory. At the same time it inaugurated a new era. From now on, the Exodus of this era must be in turn relived by Christians. Such is the rule of their liturgy and their sacraments, which are not the evocation of a bygone past, but the gift of a living presence."[19]

[19] *Op. cit.*, 16.

St. Mark's prologue (1:1-13) is, therefore, a fully coherent unity composed with great skill. Mark manages to make the reader aware of the true theological situation: the Jewish eschatological hope has found fulfillment in Jesus. This is shown by the events themselves, properly understood, and it is Mark's purpose to relate a number of incidents in such a way that they will be properly understood. Mark accomplishes here quite the same thing that the other Synoptics accomplish in their infancy narratives and John in his Prologue. He shows that Jesus is the eternal Word of God made flesh.

The activity of John the Baptist is described because John was the prophesied forerunner of the Messiah. He lived and worked in the wilderness because Isaiah had foretold this. "All the country of Judea" went out to him, "because nothing less than a national repentance would constitute the expected messianic preparation."[20] John resembles Elijah because Elijah was expected to return. John *preached* a baptism of repentance because the voice in the wilderness *cries*: "Prepare the way of the Lord." Whoever appears after John in that place and time can only be the Messiah. And in the baptism of Jesus all this receives striking confirmation not only indirectly through fulfillment of prophecy, but directly through the action of God and his Spirit, proclaiming, in the eschatological outpouring of the Spirit, Jesus to be the promised Suffering Servant.

The Wilderness theology is a theme common to all three incidents of the prologue. This prologue not only presents Jesus, the central figure of the entire book, but also characterizes his mission as a whole. The prologue incidents are not only the first acts of Jesus' ministry but a statement of Jesus' mission in terms of the Wilderness theology. All the rest of St. Mark's Gospel shows us Jesus in his confrontation with Satan and helped by God.

THE WILDERNESS PLACE

The word "wilderness" does not occur often in St. Mark's Gospel after the prologue. And where it does, in some instances it is required by the content of the passage and reveals nothing of St. Mark's Wilderness theology. But some passages are redactional and reveal Mark's approach.

[20] D. E. Nineham, *Gospel of St. Mark*, 57.

Thus Mark writes that after his baptism Jesus withdrew to Galilee and began his public ministry. The first disciples are called, the first miracles worked. Then, continues Mark: "In the morning, a great while before day, he rose and went out to a *lonely place,* and there he prayed. And Simon and those who were with him followed him, and they found him and said to him, 'Every one is searching for you'" (1:35-37).

In this and a number of similar passages, Mauser sees the persistence of the Wilderness theology throughout Mark's Gospel. And this passage does contain the essential elements of the usage. First, we see Jesus carrying out his public ministry: preaching the Kingdom, working miracles. Then he withdraws to a wilderness spot. It is there that he prays. Indeed, it is only in such wilderness spots that Mark shows Jesus praying. Then the disciples and the crowds come to seek Jesus in his wilderness retreat. It is in such wilderness areas that Jesus reveals glimpses of his hidden glory.

Jesus' exercise of his public ministry, his preaching the Kingdom and working miracles, these are simply the continuation of that struggle with the power of evil begun in the desert after his baptism. Jesus' preaching the Kingdom and his miracles represent partial victories over Satan. But Jesus' life is not to be an unbroken series of triumphs. Indeed, it is to achieve its goal only through humiliation, suffering, and apparent defeat. After the partial triumphs of his public ministry, therefore, Jesus withdraws to the wilderness. He reestablishes his identification with the wilderness: the place of testing, trial, ongoing confrontation with the power of evil. The disciples and the crowds are attracted to Jesus in the wilderness, and there they are shown glimpses of his glory. Thus they are made witnesses and partakers of this eschatological struggle with the power of evil.

After the first period of activity and the first withdrawal to a wilderness retreat, Mark goes on to sketch further public activity and describes the healing of a leper. Despite Jesus' admonition not to publicize the miracle, the man made clean "went out and began to talk freely about it, and to spread the news, so that Jesus could no longer openly enter a town, but was out *in the country*; and people came to him from every quarter" (Mark 1:45-46). Later, when the apostles return from their first missionary journey, Jesus said to them: "'Come away by yourselves to *a lonely place*, and rest a while.' For many were coming and going, and they had no leisure even to eat. And they went away to the boat to *a lonely place* by themselves. Now many saw them going, and knew them, and they ran there on foot from all the towns, and got there ahead of them" (Mark 6:31-33).

The Revised Standard Version wavers between "in the country" and "to a lonely place," but St. Mark uses one and the same term throughout, a term best translated "a wilderness-place." As in the prologue, St. Mark is more interested in the Wilderness theology than he is in giving precise geographical information. Taking the terms in their more geographical sense, the RSV translators are hard pressed to hit on a desolate spot close to Capharnaum, well cultivated at the time. In the third passage (6:31-33), St. Mark underlines his approach by twice adding the phrase "by themselves."

The three passages cited have common features. "The verses (a) are always preceded by an account of preaching and the performance of a mighty deed, (b) represent a retreat from the crowds, and (c) are followed by an account of strong attraction to Jesus on the part of the people."[21]

THE MOUNTAIN

Along with the above texts we may profitably consider several others which evoke the Wilderness concept under slightly different terms. In the first of the three passages cited above, it is said that "in the morning, a great while before day, Jesus rose and went out to a lonely place, and there he prayed" (Mark 1:35). There are only two other places in Mark which give an account of Jesus praying. After the feeding of the five thousand Jesus sent his disciples away across the lake, dismissed the crowd, "and after he had taken leave of them, he went into the hills to pray" (Mark 6:46). This prayer too seems to have taken place at night. The disciples are overtaken by a storm on their way across the lake, and "about the fourth watch of the night Jesus came to them, walking on the sea" (Mark 6:48). Again, after the Last Supper, Jesus and his apostles "went to a place which was called Gethsemane; and he said to his disciples, 'Sit here, while I pray'" (Mark 14:32).

21 Mauser, *op. cit.*, 105.

These three passages also have several notable features in common. They are the only passages in Mark which describe Jesus praying, the prayer is always at night, and the prayer is always in solitude. In the first instance (1:35), the prayer is explicitly "in a wilderness-place," while in the other two instances the mountain is seen to play the same role as wilderness. In 6:46, St. Mark writes literally, "Jesus went away *to the mountain.*" In the final instance, Gethsemane is mentioned but this garden is on the Mount of Olives.

Alongside these mountain passages wherein prayer is mentioned, we may consider some others where the mountain evokes the idea of wilderness-place and perhaps a bit more besides. After Jesus' first miracles in Galilee, St. Mark relates that "he went up into the hills and called to him those whom he desired" (3:13). Again, the text is literally, "to the mountain." After Peter's confession and the first predictions of the passion, "Jesus took with him Peter and James and John, and led them up a high mountain apart by themselves; and he was transfigured before them" (9:2). Toward the end of his life, after foretelling the destruction of the Temple, Jesus "sat on the Mount of Olives opposite the temple; then did Peter and James and John and Andrew ask him privately, 'Tell us when will this be'" (13:3-4). As can be seen, the mountain fills all the functions of the wilderness-spot, but also it is associated with moments of ultimate revelation. The Sinai traditions alone would suffice to justify this association.

The barren mountain regions easily become identical with the wilderness. What one Synoptic places in the wilderness, another places in the mountains. This circumstance may well help to interpret a line in Mark's eschatological discourse: "When you see the desolating sacrilege set up where it ought not to be . . . let those who are in Judea flee to the mountains" (13:14). Since the final, divine deliverance was expected to take place in the wilderness (mountain), their flight could be an act of repentance, a return to the desert, rather than a search for refuge.

PREPARATIONS FOR THE JOURNEY

As Jesus' self-disclosure unfolded, he also set about laying the foundations of the Church that was to carry on his work after his departure, applying the power of his redemptive sacrifice to the souls of men until he should come again at the consummation of all things. Thus we read in Mark that as Jesus went about among the villages of Galilee teaching, "he called to him the twelve, and began to send them out two by two, and gave them authority over the unclean spirits" (6:7). The twelve are made to share in his confrontation with the power of evil.

Then Mark records the instructions that Jesus gave the twelve for their missionary journeys: "He charged them to take nothing for their journey except a staff; no bread, no bag, no money in their belts; but to wear sandals and not put on two tunics" (6:8). There is a notable variation in the other Synoptics. Matthew has, "Take no gold . . . nor sandals, nor a staff" (10:9), while Luke has "no staff" (9:3). Uppermost in St. Mark's mind was the instruction given to the Israelites on the eve of the Exodus from Egypt. They were commanded to eat the paschal lamb in haste, "your loins girded, your sandals on your feet, and your staff in your hand" (Exod. 12:11).

As Mauser points out: "The missionary instruction to the disciples is given in accordance with the instruction given to Israel at the outset of her wanderings through the desert. The injunction to the disciples to carry neither bread nor bag, which is simply the bread container, can consequently be understood in analogy to the wilderness situation of Israel. As Israel was fed in the desert with manna which she could not herself provide, so the disciples are to be kept alive with nourishment for which they do not have to take thought themselves" (p. 133f).

When the apostles returned from their journey, Jesus said to them, "'Come away by yourselves to a lonely place, and rest a while.' . . . And they went away in the boat to a lonely place by themselves" (Mark 6:31-32). The withdrawal to the wilderness-spot after a period of missionary activity is strongly emphasized. Then the attraction of the crowd to the same wilderness-spot is put no less emphatically: "Now many saw them going, and knew them, and they ran there on foot from all the towns, and got there ahead of them" (6:33).

And when Jesus came ashore, "he saw a great throng and he had compassion on them, because they were like sheep without a shepherd" (6:34). This constitutes a strong allusion to a line of Old Testament thought that is extraordinarily rich in Wilderness

meaning. After he was told that he was to die outside the promised land, Moses asks the Lord to appoint a leader in his stead,
"that the congregation of the Lord may not be as sheep which
have no shepherd" (Num. 27:17). And Joshua is appointed in
Moses' place. It will be his task to lead Israel out of the wilderness into Canaan, where the people will find rest.

But not all Israel's shepherds proved faithful. After the great
national disasters, in postexilic times we find the prophet Ezekiel
denouncing the corrupt rulers of Israel as false shepherds of God's
flock. Instead of feeding the sheep, the false shepherds prey upon
them. "You have fed off their milk, worn their wool, and slaugh-
tered the fatlings. . . . So they were scattered, because there was
no shepherd and they became food for all the wild beasts. My
sheep were scattered, they wandered over all the mountains and
on every high hill" (34:3, 5-6).

The evil shepherds therefore are to be deposed from their
office and God himself will seek out his sheep. "In good pastures
will I pasture them, and on the mountain heights of Israel shall
be their grazing ground. . . . I myself will pasture my sheep; I
myself will give them rest, says the Lord God. The lost I will
seek out, the strayed I will bring back, the injured I will bind up,
the sick I will heal, shepherding them rightly" (34:14-16).

Particularly significant are the Lord's declarations recorded in
this same thirty-fourth chapter: "I will set up over them one shepherd, my servant David, and he shall feed them: he shall feed
them and be their shepherd. And I, the Lord, will be their God,
and my servant David shall be prince among them. I, the Lord,
have spoken" (34:23-24).

And when this new Joshua comes, the wilderness itself will lose
its chaotic aspects. The desert will be transformed into verdant
pastures. The people of God will not have to wait for their entrance into the promised land to find rest. They will find their
rest in the transformed wilderness itself. So the Lord declares:
"I will make with them a covenant of peace and banish wild
beasts from the land, so that they may dwell securely in the wilderness and sleep in the woods" (v. 25).

It is significant then that after the apostles' missionary journey,
Jesus invites them "to come away by yourselves to a lonely place,
and rest a while" (Mark 6:31). Then it will not escape us that
the names Joshua and Jesus mean the same thing ("The Lord

saves"), that Jesus is the Son of David, and that he declared: "I
am the good shepherd" (John 10:11). Jesus the Messiah establishes the eschatological rest of Israel in the desert. This is a line
of thought that receives further development in the story of the
feeding of the five thousand which follows.

BREAD IN THE WILDERNESS

After determining how many loaves and fishes were on hand,
Jesus "commanded them all to sit down by companies upon the
green grass. So they sat down in groups, by hundreds and by
fifties" (Mark 6:39-40). We have seen from the beginning that
the concept of the wilderness is broad enough to include pastures
sufficient for the grazing of flocks, at least in the spring. Yet
Jesus' calling the apostles aside to "rest a while" in the wilderness (v. 31), combined with this description of the people seated
on the green grass in companies of hundreds and fifties, indicates
something more than a circumstantial detail. St. Mark is thinking
of that special aspect of the Wilderness tradition we have just
met with in Ezekiel — the metamorphosis of the wilderness in the
eschatological time into a place of refreshment, life, and joy.

The people seated by companies of hundreds and fifties evokes
the order of the Mosaic camp in the wilderness. And, as we have
seen, the Qumran literature also speaks of the community as so
ordered. "The Qumran manuscripts show that this division of the
camp can assume the meaning of the order of people assembled
in the desert in expectation of the eschatological event (see pp.
60f). If this concept underlies Mark 6:39f, the multitude is characterized as the recipient of the Messianic grace which comes
to pass in the desert consummating the second exodus."[22]

In a wilderness spot Jesus, the new leader or shepherd of the
pilgrim people of God, feeds the newly pledged new Israel with
miraculous food, as Moses had done before him. In describing
this incident Jesus cannot close his mind to another meal, the
Last Supper, and he makes use of manifest eucharistic terms.
And the new dispensation surpasses the old. Jesus is himself the
feeder of the new Israel in the wilderness locale and though
the food he gives is also for physical satisfaction, it is mainly a
prefiguring of the Eucharist.

[22] *Ibid.*, 137.

"The essence of the miracle consisted in providing abundant food (more exactly loaves) in the wilderness; but this was precisely what God had done in the course of rescuing his people from Egypt by that great act of salvation which was the basic foundation of Israel's history, and the central theme of its Law."[23] After describing the feeding of the five thousand, John records that, after they had seen the miracle, the people exclaimed: "This is indeed the prophet who is come into the world" (6:14). Jesus' action puts the people in mind of the earlier bread in the wilderness.

They would also recall that the great prophet Elisha had distributed twenty barley loaves and a little fresh grain among one hundred men, so that "they ate, and had some left" (2 Kings 4:44). Jesus' action was "the fulfillment of the Law and the prophets." Jesus is the one sent by God to usher in the salvation to which the Law and the prophets had pointed forward. And if Jesus' action recalled the past, it pointed to the future also. The Christian reader would have been bound to notice that Jesus' actions as described by Mark are exactly the same as his actions at the Last Supper. "Indeed to the early Christians the whole story would have been strongly reminiscent of their eucharistic worship, at which they too sat in orderly fashion while deacons brought round to them loaves blessed and broken by the celebrant."[24]

STILLING OF THE STORM

After the feeding of the five thousand, the disciples got into the boat to go to Bethsaida, while Jesus "went into the hills to pray" (Mark 6:46). About the fourth watch of the night in the midst of a storm Jesus came to them walking on the sea. He reassures the frightened disciples ("Take heart, it is I" — Mark 6:50) and when he got into the boat the wind ceased. This passage brings to mind an earlier "stilling of the storm" in Mark (4:35-41). In this instance Jesus was asleep in the boat with the disciples. When he was awakened, Jesus "rebuked the wind, and said to the sea, 'Peace! Be still!'" (v. 39).

In his account of Jesus' temptation St. Mark reports no con-

[23] Nineham, *op. cit.*, 178.
[24] *Ibid.*, 179.

cluding victory, for he wishes to indicate that Jesus' confrontation
with Satan continues throughout the remainder of his ministry.
Every time Jesus casts out a devil he works a limited victory
over Satan, an anticipation of his ultimate victory through resurrection.

It is possible to detect interesting parallels between the account of Jesus' casting out of demons and Jesus' stilling of the
storm. Jesus rebukes the wind (Mark 4:39) and Jesus rebukes
unclean spirits (Mark 1:25; 9:25). Both the sea and unclean
spirits are commanded, "Be silent" (Mark 4:39; 1:25). Jesus'
stilling of the sea in Mark 4 is followed by the healing of the
Gerasene demoniac. Behind the use of water stands the old Near
Eastern mythology of Tiamat. As Professor Nineham writes in
the Pelican Commentary: "According to a myth which was widespread in antiquity, and was shared at one time by the Jews, the
original act of creation involved God in a desperate, but finally
victorious, contest with the forces of chaos and evil, which were
identified with, or at any rate located in, the waters of the sea." [25]

This cast of thought has a number of consequences which lend
deep meaning to Jesus' stilling the storm. Ability to control the
sea and subdue tempests was regarded as one of the characteristics of divine power. This thought comes quite frequently in
the psalms, as in Psalm 89:1: "Who is mighty as thou art, O
Lord, . . . Thou dost rule the raging of the sea; when its waves
rise, thou stillest them" (vv. 8-9). The image of a storm, or of
great waters, was frequently used as a metaphor for the evil forces
active in the world, and particularly for the tribulations of the
righteous, from which only the power of God could save them.
The complete confidence in God that the religious man ought
always display can be expressed by saying that even in the most
terrible storm he will not doubt God's power and determination to
save him.

Other aspects of Old Testament thought also lend meaning
to Jesus' stilling the storm. Thus the ability to sleep peacefully
and untroubled is a sign of perfect trust in the sustaining and pro-
tective power of God. In Psalm 3 we read: "I lie down and sleep;
I wake again, for the Lord sustains me" (v. 5), and in the
familiar Compline psalm: "In peace I will both lie down and
sleep; for thou alone, O Lord, makest me dwell in safety" (4:8).

[25] *Ibid.*, 146.

"But there were sometimes moments of national and personal disaster when it hardly seemed possible to have such trust, when it almost seemed as if God had lost interest in his people, and had ceased to watch over them. At such times they would speak of God as being 'asleep' and they did not hesitate to call upon him to 'wake up' and busy himself to help them."[26]

The Sea and the Wilderness themes, therefore, are closely akin. They both contain the aspect of chaos. Only the motif of the demons is not found in the concept of the Sea. The tendency of Jewish thinking in the centuries preceding Christ to enhance the transcendence of God and to deepen the dualism between heaven and earth resulted in the belief in mediating creatures. In the New Testament times the manifestations of chaos and death become dwelling-places for the demons. This is true both of the wilderness and of the sea. A retreat to the sea can be a retreat to the wilderness, at least in a redactionary passage. "The withdrawals to the wilderness area and to the sea are deliberate moves into the sphere of forces which manifest hostility toward God and are, therefore, the battleground for the Son of God who has come to destroy them."[27]

THE TRANSFIGURATION

The association of the Wilderness and Mountain concepts is especially evident in the Transfiguration, and these concepts are vital for an understanding of the passage. It is evident that the Exodus account of Moses on Mount Sinai (Exod. 24:12-18) and the Synoptic account of Jesus on the Mount of Transfiguration (Mark 9:2-8) are strikingly similar. Moses withdraws from the people and the elders. Taking three men with him (Aaron, Nadab, and Abihu, Exod. 24:1), Moses went up the mountain; the cloud covers the mountain; the glory of the Lord settled on the mountain; on the seventh day the Lord spoke from the cloud; when Moses came down from the mountain, his face shone so that he put a veil over it. Similarly, "after six days" Jesus, taking three apostles with him, ascended the mountain, and is transfigured before them.

In 9:1, just before the Transfiguration scene, St. Mark records

---

[26] *Ibid.*, 147.
[27] Mauser, *op. cit.*, 128.

Jesus as saying: "There are some standing here who will not taste death before they see the kingdom of God come in power." It seems almost beyond dispute that Mark regards the Transfiguration as the fulfillment of this prophecy, at least in part. "The kingdom of God come in power," says Cranfield, "is a not unfair description of what the three saw on the mount of Transfiguration. For the Transfiguration points forward to, and is as it were a foretaste of, the Resurrection, which in turn points forward to, and is a foretaste of the Parousia; so that both the Resurrection and the Parousia may be said to have been proleptically present in the Transfiguration. Compare Barth's statement: 'In His Transfiguration they saw Him proleptically as the Risen One, in it they recognized transiently the Kingdom come in power, which afterwards in His Resurrection they recognized definitively, but thereby they recognized also already — *in parte pro toto* as *arrabon* and *aparche* — precisely that which in the Parousia as in its universal revelation will become recognizable and be recognized comprehensively and finally as His glory' (K.D.III/2, p. 600)."[28] In 2 Peter also (1:16-18) the Transfiguration is thought of as proclaiming "the power and coming of our Lord Jesus Christ," i.e., it is the foreshadowing of the Parousia of the Son of Man.

The six days would correspond to Moses' six days on Mount Sinai before the Lord called him into the midst of the cloud. In both instances the six days designate a time of preparation for the reception of revelation. St. Mark says that Jesus "was transfigured before them" (9:2), while Matthew and Luke refer specifically to the transfiguration of Jesus' face (Matthew: "his face shone like the sun"; Luke: "his countenance was altered"). These latter versions, of course, heighten the resemblance to Moses on Sinai: "As he came down from the mountain, Moses did not know that the skin of his face shone because he had been talking with God" (Exod. 34:29).

MESSIANIC GLORY OF JESUS

Taken in its context in Mark, the general significance of the Transfiguration is quite clear. At Caesarea Philippi the disciples formally declared that Jesus was the Messiah. In turn Jesus taught

[28] Cranfield, *op. cit.*, 288.

them about the way this Son of Man Messiah was to accomplish his work — through suffering. In the Transfiguration the truth of the disciples' affirmation is confirmed. Jesus appears in a glory that can only be messianic. And it is shown that Jesus' declaration that he must suffer is fully in accordance with God's will. The voice out of the cloud declares: "This is my beloved Son; listen to him" (Mark 9:7).

The three disciples are given a glimpse of Jesus in that final state of Lordship and glory to which he would eventually be exalted. The reference to Elijah and Moses points in this direction. It was expected that various prominent figures of Old Testament history would reappear in the end time. As is evident from the book Malachi, Elijah came to occupy the first place in this connection. It was also expected that false prophets would appear in the last days. In the Transfiguration Moses and Elijah, the great representatives of the Law and the Prophets, bear witness that Jesus is the true Messiah. Then the voice from the clouds (which can only be God's voice) makes it clear that Jesus is the prophet of the last days whom Moses had foretold as superseding himself. Indeed, he is the Lord's "beloved Son." With his coming the Law and the Prophets are fulfilled and the old covenant is superseded by a new one.

Furthermore, both Moses and Elijah are preeminently men of the wilderness. This is self-evident in Moses' case, while Elijah, a native of Tishbeh in Gilead, could be recognized by his garment of haircloth and girdle of leather (2 Kings 1:7-8). "As prophets in the wilderness Elijah and Moses are companions of Jesus, whose work was inaugurated in the wilderness at the baptism of John and whose way, driven by the Spirit, was to be a way through the desert. The great men of the wilderness stand by his side, testifying to the character of his life and mission as the wanderer through the wilderness."[29]

Expressed in terms of the Exodus or Wilderness theology, the role of Moses and Elijah is to reveal the character of Jesus as the one in whom the prediction of the second Exodus becomes a reality. It is interesting to note that in his report of the Transfiguration, St. Luke not only mentions the fact that Moses and Elijah appeared and talked with Jesus but also gives the subject

[29] Mauser, *op. cit.*, 116.

of the conversation. They "spoke of his departure (literally, *exodus*), which he was to accomplish at Jerusalem" (9:31). There is an essential connection between the Wilderness theme and Jesus' passion.

Jesus' Transfiguration, on "a high mountain apart by themselves," takes on its full meaning when viewed in its place in the Wilderness theology. "The epiphany of the glory of God is an indispensable element of the desert tradition. In the case of both Moses and Elijah it serves as divine vindication of their mission during their life in the wilderness. The same is true of Jesus. His mission had started with his baptism in the desert. There the voice of God had declared him to be his beloved Son (1:11). Now, at the transfiguration on the wilderness mountain, this voice is heard again and the metamorphosis is the revelation of the hidden quality of Jesus' life. The lonely Galilean understands John's call to repentance as the call to a life of persistence in the desert. The obedience to this call is now vindicated by God on the way through the wilderness."[30]

The cloud and the voice out of the cloud, of course, are important elements of the Wilderness tradition. In the wilderness of Sinai, "the Lord went before them by day in a pillar of cloud to lead them along the way" (Exod. 13:21). The cloud both indicates God's guiding, protecting presence and at the same time bespeaks his transcendence, the insufferable brightness of his glory which must be veiled. The Lord called to Moses out of the cloud. Indeed, the association of cloud and voice is distinctive of the Exodus stories of the Pentateuch. In later Jewish writings, the cloud was *par excellence* the vehicle of God's *Shekinah* and the medium in and through which he manifested himself. And in view of their beliefs about the past, it was natural for the Jews to include a cloud-manifestation of God in their expectations of the end. The Son of Man manifests himself on the clouds and the early Christians certainly thought that it was in this way that Christ would appear at his final coming.

The voice from the cloud can only be that of God, who proclaims: "This is my beloved Son; listen to him" (Mark 9:7). As happened at the baptism, Jesus' mission is defined in terms of the messianic expectation of the psalms and the Suffering Servant poems of Second Isaiah, at the same time intimating a unique

[30] *Ibid.,* 117.

sonship. The phrase "listen to him" is a telling one. It is an allusion to Deut. 18:12, where Moses says: "The Lord your God will raise up for you a prophet like me from among you, from your brethren — him you shall heed." Jesus is this Second Moses, come to guide the New Israel through the new, definitive exodus.

THE LORD'S TENTING WITH HIS PEOPLE

After the vision, St. Peter says: "Let us make three booths." And St. Mark goes on to say: "For he did not know what to say" (9:5-6), indicating that Peter's proposal sprang from some misinterpretation of the event. Whatever else may be said about it, it seems clear that Mark regards Peter's suggestion as an inappropriate response to the situation, springing from a desire to prolong the experience.

Peter's suggestion is that they make three "booths" (*skene*). The English words *tent, tabernacle,* and *booth* are variant translations for the same Greek word (*skene*). *Skene* often designates the Tent of Meeting which Moses used to pitch outside the camp and where he used to commune with God (Exod. 33:7-11). The Tent of Meeting was the meeting-place of Yahweh and Moses during Israel's wilderness period. It may be precisely this that Peter has in mind. In this case the thought would be, as Mauser points out: "Peter thinks it is good to be there because he knows he stands among personages of a heavenly quality who mediate the kingdom of God to earth, and he suggests erecting tents because he wishes duration for the presence of these heavenly men so that again there may be 'tents of meeting' between the realm of heaven and the sphere of earth. It is this wish for duration which qualifies his answer to the vision as a misunderstanding. What he saw was the mystery of the resurrection (9:9), a disclosure of what was going to be the vindication of the glory of God for superseding the glory revealed at Mount Sinai" (p. 113f).

On the other hand, *skene* was also used to designate a booth (*sukkah*), a shelter made of intertwined branches or twigs such as were used in the Feast of Tabernacles. Whatever its origin may have been, the Feast of Tabernacles did come to be looked upon as a commemoration of Israel's pilgrim existence in the wilderness. But as happens so often, the festival became not only a commemoration of the past but a portent of the future.

As Professor Nineham writes in his commentary on St. Mark: "In contemporary Judaism the day of salvation was often pictured as a day when God would once more *pitch his tent* with his people as he had done during the forty years in the wilderness. The Jewish Feast of Tabernacles itself had acquired an eschatological significance, not only looking back to the tent-dwelling of the wilderness days (Lev. 23:42f) but also forward to the new age when God would again 'tabernacle' there (Zech. 14:16-19). God and his people would 'tabernacle' together."[31]

The Christians too made large use of this aspect of Exodus tradition. The image of tent-dwelling figures prominently in their thought about the new age. St. Paul tells the Corinthians that "if the earthly tent we live in is destroyed, we have a building from God, a house not made with hands" (2 Cor. 5:1). The book of Revelation speaks of the New Jerusalem as "the dwelling of God with men" (Apoc. 21:3), and, as we shall see in the next part of this study, St. John makes very important and very subtle use of this imagery in his Gospel. St. Mark too seems to have understood Peter's words eschatologically — as an offer to build the sort of dwellings God and Christ were expected to share with men in the age to come. In that case what Peter was overlooking was that this scene was not the parousia, but only its foreshadowing. Before the end, there remained much to be done and much to be suffered both by Jesus and by his disciples. That suffering is not to be by-passed or evaded, as Peter here seems to think.

In the previous episode, when Jesus began to teach the disciples "that the Son of Man must suffer many things . . . Peter took him, and began to rebuke him" (Mark 8:31-32). So Mauser too concludes: "To be sure, the way through the wilderness has not yet reached its termination in the transfiguration. This precisely is the misunderstanding of Peter who, in suggesting that tents be erected, implies that he regards the time as fulfilled and the goal of the eternal sabbath as accomplished. . . . The time in the wilderness has not yet come to an end, rather it is still to culminate in Jesus' suffering and death."[32] It is interesting to note that in his report of the Transfiguration, St. Luke not only mentions the fact that Moses and Elijah appeared and talked with

---

[31] *Op. cit.*, 236f.
[32] *Op. cit.*, 117f.

Jesus but also gives the subject of the conversation. They "spoke of his departure (literally, *exodus*), which he was to accomplish at Jerusalem" (Luke 9:31). Thus for the first time the Wilderness theme is applied explicitly to Jesus' passion and death.

From the time of Jesus' baptism it has been evident that he accepted a wilderness mission, repentance, and not only as an individual but as the Son of God, the new corporate Israel. Trial, temptation, and suffering formed a part of the wilderness existence for the first Israel in the wilderness of Sinai. They will characterize the mission of the New Israel in an even higher degree. As Jesus progressively manifests himself this becomes increasingly clear. But even the apostles and Jesus' most intimate disciples found it difficult to follow Jesus along this way.

This kingdom had been given to them, the poor; they had been given the secret of the kingdom of God, while for those outside everything was in riddles. And yet Jesus repeatedly complains of their lack of understanding. He has determined to perdure in the way of the wilderness which can only culminate in his passion and death. "The unwillingness to endure tribulation and persecution, the care for security in the world — in one word, the willingness to suffer, is the real cause of the disciples' blindness. . . . Temptation for Mark consists in the first place in the force which the fear of suffering exercises over man. Therefore, Jesus' determination to persist in the desert, expressed in the prologue, finds its conclusion in his decision to suffer and to die. On the other hand, the disciples are scared away from a proper understanding of their master through fear of enduring evil. They wish to evade the wilderness which is the home of temptation. Their lives are not marked by the decisive beginning which in the prologue was described as the commencement of Christ's mission. The basic cause of their disbelief is their determination to run away from the desert."[33]

GETHSEMANE

After the Last Supper Jesus and his apostles "went to a place which was called Gethsemane; and he said to his disciples, 'Sit here, while I pray'" (Mark 14:32). This is one of the three passages in St. Mark which give an account of Jesus praying, and as

[33] *Ibid.*, 123.

in the other instances the prayer is at night and in the wilderness (here, on the mountain). The struggle with evil which began in the desert after his baptism, continued throughout his ministry, is now approaching its decisive hour. The agony in the Garden is one of the most revealing incidents in this long struggle for the redemption of mankind.

When Jesus entered the Garden he "began to be greatly distressed and troubled" (Mark 14:33). He told the three disciples with him: "My soul is very sorrowful, even to death" (v. 34). Falling to the ground he prays that "the hour" might pass from him, that "this cup" might be removed from him. Returning to his disciples he finds them sleeping and admonishes them again to pray, "that you might not enter into temptation" (v. 38). The hour, the cup, the temptation are all recognized figures of God's judgment. This is the cup from which he is to drink, the baptism with which he is to be baptized (cf. Mark 10:38), symbolized already by his reception of John's baptism. Jesus is accepting this judgment on the behalf of others. Yet he understands the full horror of sin and death, as no other could. And knowing that his decisive confrontation with that horror was at hand, he is in agony.

In his essay, "Immortality of the Soul or Resurrection of the Dead?"(*Immortality and Resurrection*: New York, 1965), Oscar Cullmann cites the contrast between the death of Socrates and the death of Jesus. Socrates was composed, almost gaily serene. Jesus is distressed and troubled, and sorrowful even unto death. This bespeaks Jesus' perfect humanity and his complete understanding of what death really is. For him death is not something divine; it is something dreadful. "Jesus knows that in itself, because death is the enemy of God, to die means to be utterly forsaken. Therefore he cries to God; in the face of this enemy of God he does not want to be alone. He wants to remain as closely tied to God as he had been throughout his whole earthly life. For whoever is in the hands of death is no longer in the hands of God, but in the hands of God's enemy. At this moment, Jesus seeks the assistance, not only of God, but even of his disciples" (p. 16).

The author of the Epistle to the Hebrews writes that "in the days of his flesh, Jesus offered up prayers and supplications, with loud cries and tears, to him who was able to save him from death" (Heb. 5:7).

THE WILDERNESS PATTERN

In Mark, therefore, the wilderness passages follow descriptions of the teaching and healing ministry of Jesus or his disciples. The activity represents the accomplishment of Jesus' mission — the confrontation will not be an unbroken series of successes, triumphs. Quite the contrary. As Jesus' self-disclosure unfolds, it becomes increasingly clear that Jesus must fulfill his mission by way of vicarious sacrifice, and that for him the way to victory runs through humiliation, suffering, death, and apparent total defeat.

After the successful performance of his teaching and healing ministry, Jesus withdraws to the wilderness — the place where his mission properly began and which indicates his ongoing confrontation with evil. Individual miracles are not final triumphs. And as the ministry progresses, the description of limited triumphs gives way to the prediction of suffering and death, revealing that the way through the wilderness is the way to the Cross.

And, finally, we note in St. Mark that when Jesus withdraws to the wilderness, the multitudes are strongly attracted and press out to join him. And it is in Wilderness spots that the multitudes are given a glimpse of the hidden glory of the Son of Man, as at the multiplication of the loaves and the Transfiguration. All the epiphany scenes in Mark take place in wilderness-spots. In this way they are "made witnesses and partakers of the eschatological struggle between Jesus and evil at the places which indicate this continual fight."[34] The apostles' call to their office came in a Wilderness spot and is indicative of the basic condition of their mission.

Unless this reconstruction is terribly wide of the mark, the Wilderness theme is basic to St. Mark's Gospel. The other two Synoptics, of course, adopt their own positions regarding the Wilderness theme and these positions have their own stories to tell. Matthew tones down the Wilderness theme radically. Some Wilderness references are omitted altogether while others are

[34] *Ibid.*, 143.

changed into proper topographical notations. We saw earlier,[35] in Mark the wilderness is mentioned not in order to give geographical fixture to the record but to fix Jesus in the Wilderness tradition. Mark makes no attempt to designate a precise location. Matthew and Luke were not satisfied with this indefiniteness and give more precise references to locality ("wilderness of Judea," "region about the Jordan").

Matthew eliminates most of the wilderness elements from his report of the feeding of the five thousand. And there is every reason to believe that this was done deliberately. When Matthew's Gospel was receiving its final form, the Church found herself in an entirely new situation. It is highly significant that in Jesus' apocalyptic discourse Matthew alone records the words: "If they say to you, 'Lo, he is in the wilderness,' do not go out" (24:26). The Wilderness is the place of eschatological realization. Evidently a situation has arisen where Matthew found it necessary to warn Christians against any kind of eschatological expectation except the final coming of the Son of Man. The Qumran community continued to support the Wilderness tradition. The intense eschatological expectation both before and after the destruction of Jerusalem must have presented the infant Church with many problems. Matthew evidently found it necessary to speak out against the Wilderness tradition.

St. Luke shows the same negative attitude toward the Wilderness tradition. John, the last of the prophets, receives the word of God and works in the wilderness, while Jesus, with whose coming the Kingdom also came, carries on his ministry outside the wilderness. The wilderness has become the symbol of the old dispensation superseded by Jesus.

The conception of Jesus as the eschatological prophet is part of the Wilderness theology. Consequently it is interesting to note what Cullmann says regarding this conception as a solution to the Christological problem in the New Testament.[36] The conception of Jesus as prophet has definite advantages. It takes into consideration the unique and unrepeatable character of Jesus' work and it takes the human character of Jesus fully into account. It does not contain anything which contradicts the nature and goal of Jesus' work, it lends itself to combination with other es-

[35] *Supra*, 65.
[36] *Christology of the New Testament*, 13–43.

sential Christological concepts, and it is the only one which suggests the expectation of a second coming of Jesus to earth.

On the other hand, the conception has a number of disad-
vantages. It emphasizes too strongly only one side of Jesus' work,
his preaching activity. There is no room for a present function
of the eschatological Prophet. According to the Jewish expectation, the Kingdom of God will come immediately after the returned prophet has finished his preaching of repentance. And it
is difficult to connect the Prophet with a future consummation,
since the Prophet is essentially one who prepares. The conception excludes an interim after Easter. The Prophet's work is to
prepare and therefore his work cannot be the center of time;
this is opposed to the distinctly Christian outlook that the decisive thing has already happened but the consummation is yet to
come. It was only in certain heretical branches of early Jewish
Christianity that a Christological system was built entirely on
this conception, and it was through them that this approach seems
to have passed into Islam.

St. Paul

It would seem, then, that the Wilderness theme is one of the
basic themes of the Gospel of St. Mark, the earliest of the Gospels
in their present form. And in St. Paul's writings we can trace the
theme back to an even earlier stage. St. Paul makes use of
the Exodus-Wilderness theme in his first letter to the Corinthians.
And Father Boismard writes that St. Paul was "probably repeating a theme from the baptismal catechesis that was well known
to his hearers."[37]

Writing to his converts at Corinth, St. Paul warns them not to
presume upon the graces of baptism. They are still in the wilderness, and like their forefathers in the wilderness of Sinai, they
can discover that a grace abused is a liability. St. Paul draws a
parallel between baptism and the Exodus. He writes: "I want you
to know, brethren, that our fathers were all under the cloud,
and all passed through the sea, and all were baptized into Moses
in the cloud and in the sea, and all ate the same supernatural
food and all drank the same supernatural drink. For they drank

[37] J. Giblet et al., *The God of Israel, the God of Christians*, 223.

from the supernatural Rock which followed them, and the Rock was Christ. Nevertheless with most of them God was not pleased; for they were overthrown in the wilderness. . . . Now these things happened to them as a warning, but they were written down for our instruction, upon whom the end of the ages has come" (1 Cor. 10:1-5, 11).

All this happened, says St. Paul, as a warning to the Israelites in the wilderness and for the instruction of the Christians at Corinth (v. 11). The two groups find themselves in like situations. "Both the wilderness generation and the Corinthians are the recipients of divine grace (vv. 1-4). The condition of grace, however, does not provide absolute security; it can be destroyed by man's sin. At this point the analogy comes to an end. While the majority of Israelites in the wilderness fell from grace, displeased God, and were consequently destroyed (v. 5), the Corinthians are as yet only in danger of falling. They can still be warned (v. 6)."[38]

Paul pictures the Lord's gracious acts in the desert as types of the Christian sacraments. The Israelites' passage through the sea is a type of Christian baptism; the manna and water in the wilderness is a type of the bread and wine of the Eucharist. But Moses was not the real giver of life in the wilderness. Two parallel accounts of the desert wandering (Exod. 17 and Num. 20) give divergent statements about the locality of the rock struck by Moses. This divergence seems to have given rise to the legend of a wandering rock which followed the Israelites during their desert years. Identifying Jesus with this rock, St. Paul evokes the idea of the pre-existent Christ as the giver of food and drink during the desert years. So the wilderness period was a time of God's special presence, a foreshadowing of the grace enjoyed by the congregation of the new covenant.

But with most of the Israelites "God was not pleased" (1 Cor. 10:5). A grace misused can become a liability. The wilderness, the place of the Lord's special help, became a place of disaster for the Israelites. And so it is also with the Church. In this sense the Church is also in the wilderness. On this side of the end, grace can always be lost. The Israelites' experience in the desert should serve as an instruction and warning to the Corinthians. "The

[38] Mauser, *op. cit.*, 63.

Christian Church lives under grace, but not beyond temptation (1 Cor. 10:13). 'The end of the ages has come' (1 Cor. 10:11), but the new age itself has not yet arrived. The believer, indeed, lives between the times. In Christ, the new age is already a reality (2 Cor. 5:17) which can be appropriated in faith, but the old age is still the condition in which the believer lives (1 Cor. 7:31). The wilderness is a parable of this condition. As Israel was delivered from Egypt and had to pass through the desert in order to reach the promised land, so the Christian is delivered by Christ from the bondage of the old age and is on the way to the new age which in faith is already present. But to be on the way means to be subject to trial. Pride and security are, therefore, totally out of place."[39]

The wilderness is the place of test and the proving of one's faith. It is the place of expectation and pilgrimage, the place which leads from the pledges of salvation to rest in salvation. The wilderness is the place where salvation has already given pledges of its reality, but where it has not yet been manifested in its completeness.

In his study of the geographical term "Desert," J.-J. von Allmen observes that for the Church, "the desert becomes the image of the situation in which she finds herself between Pentecost and the return of Christ: salvation is there already, baptism has already effected participation in the death and resurrection of Christ, and the Lord's Supper makes it possible to taste already the heavenly gift and the powers of the world to come (Heb. 6:4f); but the Kingdom in its completeness, the Promised Land, is not yet there: salvation can yet be lost (only what you have been given can be lost!). Thus the desert becomes an image of the time in which the Church is now placed, the situation in which she must believe and love and hope, and which could be called a 'sacramental' situation. This is the theme of the Epistle to the Hebrews."[40]

During the march through the desert the Lord revealed what his ways are, what kind of a God he is. The saving acts done then established a pattern for all future saving acts. The young Church needed the Scriptures and the divine saving events of the

[39] *Ibid.*, 67f.
[40] *Companion to the Bible*, 283.

exodus and wilderness to explain the fact of Jesus. Father Guillet writes: "What meaning can Christians attach to the unique event which has turned their lives inside out? There is no other way to interpret the Christian fact but through the Old Testament. Though it seems no more than a groping in the dark, it is still a journey under the guidance of God. With love, Christians tie themselves to this history in order to understand their own experience. Amid this world of images, those which evoke the Exodus and the march in the desert hold a privileged place. Here, more than anywhere else, God Himself had acted."[41]

Christians drew upon biblical history to give meaning and names to their own experience. If they call it redemption or atonement, they both throw light on their own experience and attain a deeper understanding of the events of Israel's history. This procedure is already complete in St. Paul. Admittedly St. Paul formulates it in a somewhat baffling symbolic arrangement. Modern readers may feel that it is an abuse of a simple external resemblance — passing through water — to say that the passage through the Red Sea is a baptism. St. Paul does make use of the rabbinical methods of argumentation.

But, as Father Guillet insists, St. Paul "is infinitely more than a rabbi. He is constructing a theology. He is formulating the meaning of the event which has just transformed the world: the life, death, and resurrection of Jesus. And he is formulating this meaning in Old Testament terms. His genius consists in having isolated from the great mass of rabbinical theories their guiding lines, those which express both the structure of Israel's religion and the essential data of the religious consciousness: the role of the law and of faith, the hope of justice, the forgiveness of sins, the knowledge of God. While he attaches to external similarities the conclusive value of a sign, which nowadays astonishes us, still, in his own eyes, that is not the essential part. The essential part is that, in leaving Egypt on the word of Moses in order to bury itself in the desert under the direct guidance of Yahweh, the Hebrew people accomplished a religious effort analogous to that of the Christian who renounces the pagan world and places his existence in God's hands."[42]

[41] *Op. cit.*, 13.
[42] *Ibid.*, 14f.

HEBREWS

The desert is an image of the time in which the Church is now placed, the situation in which she must believe and hope. As was mentioned already above, this is the theme of the Epistle to the Hebrews. St. Paul used the Wilderness tradition to warn and instruct another group of unknown Christians in danger of apostasy, probably in the form of a relapse into Judaism. Let Israel's disastrous disbelief in the wilderness be a lesson to them. To evoke the desert experience the author quotes, freely, from a psalm (Ps. 95:7-11). "Today, when you hear his voice, do not harden your hearts as in the rebellion, on the day of testing in the wilderness, where your fathers put me to the test and saw my works for forty years. Therefore I was provoked with that generation, and said, 'They always go astray in their hearts; they have not known my ways.' As I swore in my wrath, 'They shall never enter my rest'" (Heb. 3:7-11).

The psalm passage evokes the principal elements of the Wilderness tradition: the wilderness as the time of grace, trial, rebellion, punishment. The entrance into Canaan is entrance into the Lord's rest. But in addition we observe the author of the psalm (David) urging his contemporaries not to neglect the movement of grace ("today") then present to them. As Paul did for the Corinthians, the author of Hebrews applies this wilderness lesson to his readers. Like the Israelites in the desert, like David's contemporaries, they too have received God's grace, their "today" has appeared. But it is both a grace and a responsibility. So the author writes: "Exhort one another every day, as long as it is called 'today,' that none of you may be hardened by the deceitfulness of sin" (Heb. 3:13).

For the Israelites in the desert, for David's contemporaries, for the readers of Hebrews, failure to cooperate with the Lord's grace is punished by exclusion from the Lord's rest. Of any of these it can be said that the "good news . . . the message which they heard did not benefit them because it did not meet with faith in the hearers" (Heb. 4:2). For the Israelites in the wilderness the Lord's rest would follow after their entrance into the promised land.

On the eve of the conquest Joshua exhorted his men saying: "Remember the word which Moses the servant of the Lord com-

manded you, saying, 'The Lord your God is providing you a place
of rest, and will give you this land'" (Josh. 1:13). But by that
time many had died in the wilderness. "And to whom did he
swear that they shall never enter his rest, but to those who were
disobedient?" (Heb. 4:18). But since the Israelites "who formerly
received the good news failed to enter because of disobedience,
again he sets a certain day, 'Today'" (Heb. 4:6-7). This is the
new opportunity that David proclaimed in his time.

The Lord set another "Today" long after the conquest, as David
proclaims in the psalm, "for if Joshua had given them rest, God
would not speak later of another day" (Heb. 4:8). The readers of
Hebrews have been given their own day and it remains to be
seen whether they will use it better than those favored in former
ages. Will they at length enter the Lord's rest? "For good news
came to us just as to them; but the message which they heard
did not benefit them, because it did not meet with faith in the
hearers. For we who have believed enter that rest" (Heb. 4:2-3).

Now, indeed, the full nature of the Lord's rest has at length
been revealed. This is a far greater rest than the enjoyment of
Canaan's fertility, this is the true fulfillment of the rest that King
David spoke of. This rest is nothing other than a participation of
the Lord's rest. "We who have believed enter that rest . . . although his works were finished from the foundation of the world"
(Heb. 4:3). The rest that neither Joshua nor David could give,
the new Joshua (Jesus) gives to those who have faith in him.
"For if Joshua had given them rest, God would not speak later
of another day. So then, there remains a sabbath rest for the
people of God; for whoever enters God's rest also ceases from his
labors as God did from his. Let us therefore strive to enter that
rest, that no one fall by the same sort of disobedience" (Heb.
4:8-11).

The Christian too is in the wilderness, looking forward with
confidence to his entrance into the Lord's rest. Christians are the
"wandering people of God," wayfarers to eternal rest. The Christian's true home is in "the world to come" (Heb. 2:5), the new
age ushered in by the gospel. On this earth Christians have no
lasting city, but "seek the city which is to come" (Heb. 13:14). In
this present age Christians are strangers and exiles wandering
to their true homeland.

C.F.D. Moule observes that more than any other part of the

New Testament, the Epistle to the Hebrews presses into service the Platonic conception (adopted also by Philo) of a supra-sensible world of absolute reality over against a sensible world which is only its reflection or copy. Yet this shadow-world is not so Platonic but that in it the decisive saving acts of history take place. "The writer to the Hebrews makes bigger concessions to Greek ways of expression than Paul or John; but there is never a doubt but that, in common with all apostolic Christianity, he takes time seriously and thinks of history as significant and of this world as an important arena of divine action." [43]

But for the moment, the lesson is to be drawn from the not-yet-realized aspect of the Kingdom. Let the Hebrews recall the time when they withstood persecution and accepted the plundering of their property, knowing that they "had a better possession and an abiding one" (Heb. 10:34). Let them live by faith, "the assurance of things hoped for, the conviction of things not seen" (Heb. 11:1).

It was by faith that the great men of old received divine approval — Abel, Enoch, and Noah. "By faith Noah, being warned by God concerning events as yet unseen, took heed and constructed an ark for the saving of his household" (Heb. 11:7). Above all, Abraham is the patriarch of men of faith, of those who stake their all on things unseen. It was by faith that he left his homeland and trusted God's promises to make him a mighty people. He lived as a stranger and sojourner in the land of Canaan. After Sarah's death at Hebron in the land of Canaan, Abraham went to the Hittites among whom he was living and said: 'I am a stranger and a sojourner among you; give me property among you for a burying place, that I may bury my dead out of my sight'" (Gen. 23:4).

And the author of the Epistle to the Hebrews underlines the fact that these great patriarchs never saw the fulfillment of God's promise; yet they lived as if the promise was sure, and died in faith. Thus he writes that, "all these died in faith, not having received what was promised, but having seen it and greeted it from afar, and having acknowledged that they were strangers and exiles on the earth. For people who speak thus make it clear that they are seeking a homeland. If they had been thinking of

[43] *Birth of the New Testament,* 169.

that land from which they had gone out, they would have had opportunity to return. But as it is, they desire a better country, that is, a heavenly one. Therefore God is not ashamed to be called their God, for he has prepared for them a city" (Heb. 11:13-16).

From the fact that these great patriarchs lived in Canaan as resident aliens, our author infers that the homeland which they really sought was the heavenly city prepared for them by God. Apart from this faith, they might have seized the opportunity to return to Mesopotamia. The fact that they did nothing of the kind proved the genuineness of their faith.

Paradoxically, then, Wilderness proves to be one of the most fertile concepts of Scripture. In the first place, Wilderness is one aspect of the Exodus tradition, one of the most basic in Biblical revelation. Wilderness immediately reminds us of the exodus from Egypt and the forty years that Israel spent in the desert. The prophets came to regard this wilderness period as the most significant of sacred history and often spoke of a return to the desert for purposes of purification and rededication. It was not an accident, then, that John the Baptist appeared in the desert to proclaim the eschatological realization. He preached a baptism of repentance which answers to the crossing of the Red Sea and enables the people of God to be gathered together and re-formed.

The Wilderness is the place of danger and temptation but it is also the place of special grace. Man cannot by himself live there and therefore it is here especially that his faith is tested. God's people have to choose whether they will put their trust in the Lord or whether they will wish to return "to Egypt." This is why the Wilderness is also the place of Jesus' temptation.

But, as von Allmen points out, from the desert Jesus could be transported in a moment to the heart of religion (the pinnacle of the Temple) or confronted with all the world's grandeur. Indeed, "the desert is, in a sense, the 'world' in its essential state, and it is for this reason that it is regarded as the resort of demons (Matthew 12:43; Luke 8:29; 11:24): if God leads His people and His Son there, and later on anchorites and hermits, it is not to cause them to flee from the world, but on the contrary to bring them to its heart so that there, in the hardest place of all, they may manifest His victory and His rights. It may be supposed, moreover, that when Jesus withdraws into the desert, generally after having performed a miracle (Mark 1:35; Luke 4:42; 5:16), it is not only to seek privacy (cf. Matthew 14:12f and parallels; Mark 1:44; John 11:53f), but rather to betake Himself to the place where He ought to give all the glory to God."[44]

Then, the Wilderness became the image of the situation in which the Church finds herself between Pentecost and Parousia, when the war has been won but the battle continues. And, finally, the Wilderness is "an image of the world in the sense that it is awaiting the time when it will no longer be the desert, when it will be delivered from that which makes it formidable; for the world awaits, with an ardent expectation, the cosmic baptism of the last day when it will be transformed into a new world (2 Pet. 3:13; cf. Rom. 8:18-23): the desert awaits the time when God will make it into a garden (Ps. 107:35; Is. 32:15; 35:1-7; 41:18f; 43:19f; 51:3)."[45]

The imagery of the desert years was used to illustrate the general eschatological outlook of the New Testament. Like Israel between exodus and conquest, the Church was in an interim phase, caught between fulfillment and hope. The Israelites were rescued from Egypt and brought out of the land of bondage. In one sense the great deliverance was an event of the past, but at the same time they were not yet in the promised land. "If they looked back to the crossing of the Red Sea, they exulted in a divine intervention which had already taken place; but if they looked wistfully towards the crossing of Jordan, they were aware that they were still outside the promised land. God had brought them out, but he had not yet brought them in. Thus the wilderness years provide a remarkable illustration of the situation of the Christian Church today. She looks back to the great redeeming acts of God and rejoices in the blessings they have brought to her; at the same time she earnestly looks forward to the glory which shall be revealed and to the entrance into the eternal Kingdom."[46]

[44] *Op. cit.*, 282f.
[45] *Ibid.*, 284.
[46] Glasson, *Moses in the Fourth Gospel*, 110.

Part Three

MOSES IN THE FOURTH GOSPEL

In his *Christ in the Wilderness*, Ulrich W. Mauser asserts: "In the Gospel of John the wilderness motif plays only a very insignificant role."[1] This is remarkable, since in the very next number in the same series, T. F. Glasson asserts that "In recent years increasing attention has been paid to the importance (for the understanding of the New Testament generally) of seeing the Messianic hope in terms of a new Exodus and of recognizing the Messiah as a second Moses. In the following pages it is hoped to show that this approach is one of the keys to the understanding of the Fourth Gospel. Admittedly it is only one of several, but it is an important one."[2]

Mauser lists a number of recent writings supporting the same view and comments: "All authors champion a view that the Fourth Gospel is determined in its structure by a very thoroughgoing typology of the book of Exodus. The arguments advanced seem to me without exception very forced and many details, as well as the whole thesis, are quite unconvincing."[3] Evidently the Wilderness motif is not in the Fourth Gospel in the same way it is found in Mark's Gospel. If it is there at all it is in some more allusive way.

The Brazen Serpent passage illustrates well the difference between Mauser's and Glasson's point of view. For Mauser, "that this actually happened in the wilderness is more or less accidental" (p. 76); while for Glasson, "with the brazen serpent of John 3:14 we come to a wilderness incident which is quite explicitly related to Christ and the Gospel. 'As Moses lifted up the serpent

[1] *Op. cit.*, 75.
[2] Glasson, *Moses in the Fourth Gospel*, 10.
[3] Mauser, *op. cit.*, 75, note 1.

101

in the wilderness, even so must the Son of man be lifted up, that whosoever believeth may have eternal life'" (p. 33). Actually it would seem that both Mark and John are pointing to a type – antitype relationship between the Old Testament and the New, but that their typological styles are noticeably different.

TYPOLOGY

Essays on typology by G. W. H. Lampe and K. J. Woollcombe make up one of the numbers in the *Studies in Biblical Theology* series.[4] Both authors find no difficulty in distinguishing between typology and allegory in their pure form. Typology, says Lampe, "seeks to discover and make explicit the real correspondences in historical events which have been brought about by the recurring rhythm of the divine activity" (p. 29). Allegory, on the other hand, is based not on an interpretation of history, but "on a particular quasi-Platonist doctrine of the relation of the literal sense of Scripture – the outward form or 'letter' of the sacred writings – to eternal spiritual reality concealed, as it were, beneath the literal sense" (p. 30). In allegory the literal sense is regarded not so much as conveying the inward reality but as disguising it and is dispensed with as quickly as possible. It is based on ideas about the correspondence of the earthly order as the shadow with the intelligible sphere as the reality. Pure allegory is usually concerned with moral edification rather than with pointing to Christ. Lampe regards historical typology as legitimate, allegory as misleading and harmful.

For Woollcombe, typological exegesis is "the search for linkages between events, persons or things *within the historical framework of revelation,* whereas allegorism is the search for a secondary and hidden meaning underlying the primary and obvious meaning of the narrative" (p. 40). Typology "was to the Apostolic writers, what Biblical theology is to the modern exegete – the historical approach to the understanding of the saving acts of God" (p. 69). Lampe also makes the very sensible point that we cannot ignore typology simply because the New Testament writers themselves use it. If we are to understand what the New Testament writers are trying to say, it is quite indispensable that

[4] "Essays on Typology."

we seek to retrace their thoughts, and read the Old Testament as they read it. "Typological study is necessary if we are to appreciate the meaning of the New Testament" (p. 19).

FEAR OF ALLEGORY

The authors agree in distinguishing typology and allegory, assigning the former to the realm of the historical and disapproving of the latter. But they also have to admit that St. Paul, for one, did not feel bound to adhere to a strictly historical type of typology. Furthermore it would be a mistake to attribute allegory solely to Hellenistic ideas. "The idea of the earthly counterpart to the heavenly reality can be read out of the Pentateuch as well as out of Plato," Lampe notes (p. 32). Hellenistic ideas had made a deep impression on Judaism before the Christian era.

While both authors see St. Paul's typology falling somewhere between historical typology and allegory, Woollcombe asserts on the basis of a comparison between Paul and Philo, that "there is not a trace of Platonic idealism in St. Paul's typology" (p. 67). In Paul's exegesis of the Sarah — Hagar story (Gal. 4), Hagar represents the Old Covenant and Sarah the New. In Philo, Hagar is made out to represent education, and Sarah virtue. Paul and Philo use a common typological vocabulary but in Paul the vocabulary is harnessed to the exposition of God's redemptive work in history, while in Philo it is harnessed to symbolic allegorism.

In an essay entitled "Parable, Allegory, and Mysticism," Professor E. J. Tinsley states: "The symptoms of the two great phobias are discernible in a good deal of recent Christian theology, both on the continent and in this country; these are, the obsessive fear of 'allegory' (and in some cases this includes an uneasiness with metaphor as such), and of 'mysticism.'"[5] In some instances this phobia arises from a conviction that the allegorist cannot take history seriously. This usually happens when "the moralizing dissection practised by a good deal of patristic and mediaeval exegesis of the Bible" is not sufficiently distinguished from the "distinctive character of scriptural allegories, especially those in the teaching of Jesus" (*ibid.* 154).

But in many other instances the attempt to abolish or get be-

[5] *Vindications, Essays on the Historical Basis of Christianity*, 153.

yond metaphor is "an instance of the age-old 'gnostic' distaste for the limitations, and provisional quality, of finite existence" (*ibid.* 155). "Religionless Christianity" seems to display "all the symptoms of a 'gnostic' discomfort with the actualities of human existence and an inability to stomach the idea that there is a permanent need for the finite, particular image" (*ibid.* 160). "The best that can be said for some forms of demythologization is that they sometimes come near to saying the same thing as the original but in a vaguer way" (*ibid.* 191).

Johannine Typology

John's typology does not differ greatly from Paul's — this is the conclusion that would seem to follow from a consideration of the Exodus theme in St. John. On the one hand, Mauser finds the Exodus theme in John hardly at all and Glasson regards it as one of John's main themes. The net result seems to be that the Exodus theme is in John's Gospel but that John's typology differs somewhat from that of the Synoptics. Synoptic typology is more historical and direct, more concerned with continuity than contrast between the old and the new, and it sticks closer to the broad outline of salvific patterns. John no more departs from the historical plan of salvation than Paul does, but like Paul, John does make frequent use of the earthly-heavenly, shadow-reality comparison. Usually John dwells on the contrast between the old and new, and in this regard John is distinguished from Mark especially. On the whole John's evocation of the Exodus theme is more subtle and allusive than the Synoptics', which are by no means obvious according to modern norms. Thus John not infrequently evokes the Exodus theme by nothing more than a glancing allusion to some aspect of the Wilderness tradition.

There does not seem to be any great need, then, to have recourse to borrowings from the world of Hellenistic thought in order to explain St. John's thought. Professor Moule says that he finds himself among those who detect the minimum of Hellenistic influence in the New Testament, as far as basic themes are concerned. "And, where it leaves its mark, it seems to me to be more often by way of recoil from it than acceptance of it. This is not to deny that there are numerous borrowings of words and phrases and even ideas from the Hellenic world, but these are on a level shallower than that of the basic themes. The substance is usually Hebraic, even when the terms are Hellenic."[6] It is widely recognized today that already by the time of Christ monotheistic Judaism had been penetrated by Oriental dualism, as is evident from the Qumran literature, and that possibly even a measure of Western rationalism had crept into the recesses of Hebrew thought.

The Platonic conception (adopted also by Philo) of a suprasensible world of absolute reality over against a sensible world which is only its reflection or copy is more in evidence in the Epistle to the Hebrews than it is in St. John. But even here the shadow world is not so Platonic as to call the objective reality of the history of salvation into question. "Perhaps Paul, and even John, are more firmly on the Hebrew side of the line; but Hebrews, for all its concessions, never surrenders 'the scandal of particularity.'"[7]

In his *Interpretation of the Fourth Gospel*, C. H. Dodd gives it as his opinion that "in thoughtful religious circles at the time, and circles with which Johannine thought has demonstrable affinities," the Platonic doctrine of Ideas "had entered into the texture of thought."[8] One might concur in this, perhaps, without accepting another of his contentions — that while John is partly aware of the teaching of Rabbinic Judaism, he is "only partly sympathetic to it. He is more sympathetically in touch with Hellenistic Judaism as represented by Philo."[9] Seeking the origin of Paul's doctrine of the Body of Christ, J. A. T. Robinson is led to observe that "in the hellenised Judaism of Paul's day it is very doubtful whether most people would have been interested, or able, to isolate the differing ingredients of a syncretism which had by then become thoroughly mixed."[10]

THE TRUE

What is evident is that St. John does make prominent use of the idea that the supernal world is the source of all that is true

[6] Moule, *Birth of the New Testament*, 3.
[7] *Ibid.*, 169.
[8] Cambridge, 1953, p. 139.
[9] *Ibid.*, 133.
[10] *The Body*, 56.

and real, whether we designate this as Hellenistic or not. In the Prologue already St. John, speaking of Jesus, declares that "The true light that enlightens every man was coming into the world" (1:9). And later St. John is to speak of the "true vine" and the "true bread." The visible things we see in our world are only a faint copy, a symbol, of the invisible realities. Thus the "true light" is the archetypal light, light itself, of which every visible light in this world is only a copy, a symbol. The "true bread" is the reality which lies within and behind every visible and tangible loaf, in so far as it can properly be so called. The "true vine" is, says Dodd, "that which makes a vine a vine, at once its inner essence, and the transcendental real existence which abides while all concrete vines grow and decay" (p. 140).

When this approach is brought to the interpretation of the Old Testament, some interesting results follow. For example, in one of Jeremiah's oracles the Lord declares: "I planted you a *true* vine, wholly of pure seed." The Hebrew word for "true" (*'emeth*) expresses the idea of "trustworthiness," and so the meaning is a plant which can be trusted to produce fruit after its kind. But the Hebrew term for "truth," like a number of other terms, undergoes a shift of meaning in passing into Greek. The Greek term for "true" (*alethinos*) "properly means 'real,' as opposed to that which is either fictitious or a mere copy" (p. 139). When, therefore, John speaks of "true bread," "true vine," he does at least suggest the idea of spiritual, eternal realities, of which earthly visible bread and vines are but a reflection. And John's emphasis on Jesus as the true Bread and the true Vine are a notable feature of his Gospel.

To appreciate the Exodus theme in John it is also necessary to start with a realization that John's use of Scripture is something special. At a point where no direct reference to the Exodus tradition is to be seen, Glasson writes that "it is not fanciful to suggest that in reading John, one must remember his allusiveness; one must be ready to read between the lines and to follow up hints and pointers" (p. 36). Moule writes that "in general the Jesus of the Fourth Gospel uses scripture in an allusive, poetic, evocative way."[11]

John is no less dependent upon the Old Testament than the

[11] *Op. cit.*, 66.

Synoptics, but he prefers to collect the sense of the Old Testament rather than to quote directly. Old Testament "proof" texts found in the Synoptics are not quoted verbally in the Fourth Gospel but the content of these texts has penetrated the theology of the Fourth Gospel. The evangelist does not rely mainly on quotations and proof-texts, but he has, as it were, absorbed the whole of the Old Testament into his system.

Furthermore, John on occasion plays upon the double meaning of a Greek word. In an article on "The Old Testament in the Fourth Gospel," C. K. Barrett writes that "there is no reason why he should not have made a double (or even more complicated) allusion to the Old Testament."[12] One of the evangelist's characteristic usages is to take words of dual connotation and to follow both meanings.

When the Synoptics and John deal with the same theme interesting differences often emerge. Thus, the parable of the Lost Sheep in the Synoptics may be compared with the passage about the Good Shepherd in John 10:1-18. While Matthew and Luke give slightly different applications of the parable, in both instances the parable and its application are kept simple and straightforward. The point is obvious: if a shepherd is fit to be a shepherd, that must be his attitude.

The Good Shepherd passage in John, on the other hand, is very much an allegory, the details of the story taking on separate significance. Long before the passage is at an end, the figure of the shepherd has fused with that of Jesus himself. All the details of the story are selected because they aptly symbolize aspects of his work. Characterizing John's use of Scripture as allusive, poetic, evocative, Moule goes on to say that "it is the picture-writing, the symbols of Scripture that he uses, almost as embryonic parables."[13]

In John 15:1 we hear Jesus declare: "I am the true vine." The Vine and Branches passage as a whole follows from an Old Testament preparation, where the vine or vineyard became a standing symbol for the people of God. Again the presentation is strongly allegorical, various elements taking on separate significance. C. H. Dodd writes: "The language changes to and fro between the literal and the metaphorical in a way which would be

---

[12] *Journal of Theological Studies*, 1947 (48) 155–169, 157.
[13] Moule, *op. cit.*, 66.

bewildering, if the reader were not conscious all through that all the statements made really refer to Christ and His disciples, under the symbol of a vine and its branches, rather than to any earthly vine" (p. 136). The symbol is almost absorbed in the thing signified and the allegory is chiefly to be understood out of a rich background of associations which the vine-symbol had already acquired.

So likewise with the other basic symbols that John uses: bread, water, light. In all these cases there is an Old Testament preparation which St. John presupposes. Furthermore, all these symbols were used to some degree in the world of Hellenic thought and religion and there is every reason to believe that the first readers of the Gospel would be aware of this fact. But Moule is probably right when he insists that these symbols appear in the Fourth Gospel more by way of recoil from Hellenic thought than acceptance of it.

The Exodus in the Fourth Gospel

St. John's first chapter falls into two parts: 1:1-18, commonly designated the Prologue, and 1:19-51, covering much the same ground as Mark 1:1-15, from the appearance of John the Baptist to the departure for Galilee. John has enlarged his introductory chapter by relating the "call" of four disciples, for the sake of the confirmatory testimony they afford to the Messiahship of Jesus. John brings this introductory chapter to a climax with Jesus' words to Nathanael. Nathanael was convinced by Jesus' supernatural knowledge: "When you were under the fig tree, I saw you" (John 1:48). Jesus hastens to assure him that he would see greater things than these. "And he said to him, 'Truly, truly, I say to you, you will see heaven opened, and the angels of God ascending and descending upon the Son of man'" (John 1:51).

All the rest of John's Gospel is controlled by this revelation of the Son of Man. "The whole series of 'signs' which follows, culminating in the supreme sign of the cross and resurrection, *is* the vision of the heaven opened and the angels of God ascending and descending upon the Son of Man. And these 'signs' are history. 'The Logos was made *flesh* — and we beheld His glory'" (Dodd, 294).

The second part of John's first chapter (1:19-51) corresponds to

Mark 1:4-15. Could it be, then, that John's Prologue was meant to correspond to Mark's first three verses? We have already seen how rich those verses of St. Mark's Gospel are in the Exodus theology. But the basic correspondence between the two passages seems to lie in the idea of revelation. In Mark the verses have to do with the fulfillment of prophecy: "As it is written in Isaiah the prophet, 'Behold, I send my messenger before thy face'" (Mark 1:1-2). And basically for John the Logos doctrine seems to be a way of asserting that prophecy is exhaustively realized in the gospel story, in Jesus Christ.

THE LOGOS

The origin of John's Logos doctrine has been a much disputed question. Three possible lines of explanation seem to have emerged: Greek thought about the logos, or, in the Old Testament itself, the biblical concepts of wisdom or the word of God. In making our choice, says T. W. Manson, "it is necessary to remember that the age in which the Prologue was composed was an age of eclecticism and syncretism. Men picked and chose among the floating ideas and fitted their pickings together into new forms of thought and explanation. We are therefore *not* bound to suppose that John adhered strictly to any one of the possible lines of explanation available when he wrote his prologue."[14]

Still we want to know what is fundamental to John's way of thinking. Manson's opinion is that the Old Testament "word of God" is the basis of John's Logos doctrine. "For John the 'word' is the creative and revealing word of God. And Jesus Christ is the supreme revelation of God" (*ibid.* 149). John's theology is primarily a theology of Revelation and the essence of the Gospel is that it is a full and complete revelation of the truth. "This saving revelation is the crown and fulfilment of the long course of God's dealing with the world in Creation and Revelation. God made the world by his word. His word came also to mankind through the prophets. But these revelations are partial and occasional. From each you may learn a little about God. In the revelation in Jesus we have the complete and final manifestation of

[14] *On Paul and John,* 149.

God. There the *logos* is present *in toto* and all the time, i.e., in Jesus all that *we* can know of God is made known" (*ibid.* 160).

Earlier in the same essay Manson makes the point that "the Johannine interest is not metaphysical, but, like that of the rest of the New Testament, primarily historical. He is not concerned to explain the *logos* in terms of first principles, but to show how God so loved the *kosmos* that he intervened in history for its redemption from the power of evil and death. It is an historical event and not a metaphysical theory that is being explained" (*ibid.* 136).

For Dodd too the Old Testament Word of God concept is an important source of John's Logos teaching, though he is by no means content to stop there. "I have tried to show," Dodd writes, "that whatever else the Logos of the Fourth Gospel is, on one side it is the Word of the Lord, by which the heavens were framed, which came through the prophets to Israel, was rejected by the people at large, but found acceptance with the faithful remnant, to whom it gave the status of God's children. This prophetic word, says the evangelist, was not merely fulfilled in the sense that what it declared came true. It was fulfilled in a deeper sense. The Word itself, the word which proceeds from the mouth of God and cannot return to him void, found actual embodiment, and worked creatively as at the beginning. How could the writer more impressively have stated the fundamental conviction of the apostolic *kerygma*, that the whole meaning of prophecy is exhaustively realized in the Gospel story?" (*op. cit.* 294f).

John 1:17 is a key to John's main thesis, and, characteristically, it comes in the form of a strong contrast. "The law was given through Moses; grace and truth came through Jesus Christ." What the Torah could not do, Jesus does. The Torah is but a shadow of the true Word of God, which came in its full reality in Jesus Christ.

"Grace and truth" is an essentially Old Testament phrase. Its basic meaning is suggested by the RSV translation of Exod. 34:6: "The Lord, a God merciful and gracious, slow to anger, and abounding in steadfast love and faithfulness." The two Hebrew words are closely related in meaning, signifying God's loyalty and faithfulness to his covenant and covenant people. Sometimes, as in ordinary Greek usage, *truth* in John means the Christian revelation brought by and revealed in Jesus. "This revelation arises out of the faithfulness of God to his own character, and to his promises, of which it is the fulfilment. It is saving truth (John 8:32); it is perceived only through the work of the Spirit (John 16:13), and by those who are predestined in conformity with it (John 3:21)."[15] This revelation is given not in metaphysical but in moral terms.

THE NEW MOSES

Mauser and Glasson may not be as far apart as it might appear at first. It is the Exodus theme as a structural principle in the Gospel of John that Mauser rejects. And while Glasson holds for the importance of the Exodus theme in John, the passages to which he devotes his attention do not seem to go beyond isolated instances of typology. Mauser seems to be right in rejecting the view that "the Fourth Gospel is determined in its structure by a very thorough-going typology of the book of Exodus" (*op. cit.* 75). Attempts have been made to establish a correspondence between Moses' miracles in the wilderness and certain Johannine materials (chiefly miracles), or between the Lord's (Moses') signs in Egypt and Jesus' signs.[16] These correspondences do begin to appear forced and unconvincing when they are made to serve as the main structure of the Fourth Gospel.

On the other hand, it is not farfetched to work on the supposition that John did at times intend to suggest a parallel between the events of the Exodus and the works of Christ. Father Braun, O.P., among others, has supported this contention.[17] In the tradition which prevailed among the Pharisees, says Father Braun, the Messiah was expected in the guise of a new Moses. On this score, what the Lord did through Moses in the Exodus must be reproduced in the last days. If the first liberation brought bread from heaven and water from the rock, so must the last, definitive liberation. And the Rabbis strained to multiply these parallels.

---

[15] C. K. Barrett, *Gospel according to St. John*, 139.

[16] Cf. J. Enz, "The Book of Exodus as a Literary Type for the Gospel of John," *Journal of Biblical Literature*, 76 (1957), pp. 208–15; R. Smith, "Exodus Typology in the Fourth Gospel," *Journal of Biblical Literature* 81 (1962), pp. 329–42.

[17] "*L'Evangile de saint Jean et le grandes tradition d'Israel*," IV, "*Moise et l'Exode*," Revue Thomiste (60, 2), April, 1960, pp. 165–184.

This, of course, is in accord with Moses' proclamation: "The Lord your God will raise up for you a prophet like me from among you" (Deut. 18:15). According to Second Isaiah the miracles of the first Exodus will be surpassed and forgotten.

It does seem that John chose those of Jesus' signs which show that he is the New Moses, and therefore the Promised Messiah. To make his point with the Jews, he had to meet them on their own ground. Release from Egyptian slavery was an anticipation of messianic redemption. Therefore the works by which the Messiah is recognized must be the same as those of Moses. This is John's starting point, says Braun, and where possible John takes steps to make Jesus' signs resemble those of the Exodus as much as possible.

In *The God of Israel, the God of Christians*, Father Boismard gives it as his opinion that "it is Saint John who gives the most completely developed typology of the Exodus. It is to be found on almost every page of his gospel."[18] As has been mentioned above, Glasson holds that Exodus typology is "one of the keys to the understanding of the Fourth Gospel. Admittedly it is only one of several, but it is an important one" (*op. cit.* 10). As the New Moses, Jesus leads the New Exodus. He gives a New Law far superior to that given by Moses. He gives food to the hungry multitudes in the desert. Jesus gathers "into one the children of God who are scattered abroad (John 11:52); he is the "light of the world" who goes before his people (John 8:12). Lifted up on the Cross, Jesus frees his people from the sting of death. Jesus is the true Paschal Lamb by whose blood his people are delivered.

THE LAMB OF GOD

Unlike the Synoptics, John leaves the miracles of mercy in the background. And, as Professor Marsh points out: "John handles the Exodus material as it is applied to the gospel story somewhat differently from the Synoptists. He retains only part of the opening cycle, but introduces the imagery in a new form with the Baptist's confession that Jesus is the Lamb of God (John 1:29, 35). He also changes the application at the end of the ministry, for instead of the Last Supper being the point where, as an actual Passover, Exodus meanings are applied to the death

[18] J. Giblet et al., 224.

of Christ, John tells us that Jesus died at the very hour that the Passover lambs were being slain in the Temple."[19]

Most things in John's Gospel are prepared for in the Prologue and so it is with John the Baptist. He appears as a witness in the Prologue and an historical account of his testimony follows (John 1:19-34), akin to that in the Synoptics. John is not the Christ; indeed, in sharp contrast to what is found in Matthew, he is not Elijah. Almost the personification of the witness of the Old Testament, John declares: "Behold the Lamb of God, who takes away the sin of the world!" (John 1:29).

There are several possible origins for the term "Lamb of God," and in view of John's tendency to follow up multiple lines of thought, we are not forced to pick one to the exclusion of all others. There may be reference to the lambs sacrificed daily in the Temple, or to the goats used on the Day of Atonement, one of which carried away the sins of the people into the wilderness. Jesus, the Lamb of God, "takes away the sin of the world." But two other sources seem to be more central to John's thought: the lamb mentioned in the description of the Servant of the Lord (Is. 53:7), and the Passover lamb sacrificed at the annual festival. In view of John's interest in Jesus as the true Passover, this should perhaps be given first place, although it seems impossible to exclude "the lamb that is led to the slaughter" of Isaiah, who "opened not his mouth" (Is. 53:7). And when we think of the New Testament as a whole, we cannot exclude the lamb which plays a part in apocalyptic imagery (Apoc. 14:1), and represents the Messiah, who purifies his people.

The Brazen Serpent

Although the Exodus theme is alluded to in the Prologue, it may be well to consider some of the more obvious examples of Exodus typology before turning to the more subtle allusions. And for obviousness, the Brazen Serpent passage (John 3:1-15) should probably be given first place. In his interview with Nicodemus, Jesus declares: "As Moses lifted up the serpent in the wilderness, so must the Son of man be lifted up, that whoever believes in him may have eternal life."

[19] J. Marsh, "Theology of the New Testament," in *Peake's Commentary on the Bible*, 763.

According to Dodd's division of John, the Brazen Serpent passage is in the first of the seven episodes which make up the Book of Signs, the central portion of John's Gospel. Dodd calls this first episode (2:1–4:42), "The New Beginning." It is made up of two narrative sections (the miracle of Cana, and the cleansing of the Temple), followed by two largely discourse sections (with Nicodemus, and with the Samaritan woman at Jacob's well). The common theme of the episode may perhaps best be characterized by Paul's aphorism: "The old has passed away, behold the new has come" (2 Cor. 5:17). At Cana water is replaced by wine; then in Jerusalem a new temple is foretold; the dialogue with Nicodemus is about new birth; the dialogue with the Samaritan woman contrasts Jacob's well with "living water," while over against the ancient cults of Jerusalem and Gerizim is set an hour "when the true worshippers will worship the Father in spirit and truth" (John 4:23). The episode therefore spells out what was stated in the Prologue: "The law was given through Moses; grace and truth came through Jesus Christ" (John 1:17).

Jesus tells Nicodemus, a teacher of Israel: "Unless one is born anew, he cannot see the kingdom of God" (John 3:3). Rebirth is the starting-point of the discourse. In Matthew we hear Jesus saying that "in the new world" his disciples would judge the tribes of Israel (19:28). "New world" translates *palingenesia*, literally, "regeneration, rebirth." "This was a technical term with the Stoics and in the mystery religions, but it was also used by the Hellenistic Jewish writer, Philo. . . . It refers to the kingdom as the time when everything will be new, born again, because God's will will be done on earth (Matthew 6:10)."[20] Here in John we hear Jesus declaring that this rebirth is the very condition for entrance into the Kingdom.

Nicodemus' failure to understand affords an opportunity for an explanation. It is really a question of man's passing out of the lower order of existence, the realm of flesh, into the higher order of existence, the realm of spirit in which alone eternal life is his portion. It is this passage into the higher order of existence which has been symbolized by the changing of water into wine and by the cleansing (i.e., transformation, or destruction and renewal) of the temple. The phrase "born of the Spirit" which occurs here (John 3:5, 6, 8) reflects the Prologue's "born of God"

[20] J. Fenton, *Gospel of St. Matthew*, 317.

(John 1:12-13). To be a child of God is not the result of any process comparable with that of physical birth, "of blood, of the will of the flesh, of the will of man." It is by receiving the Logos that one gains the power to be God's child. Jesus began by declaring to Nicodemus that "Unless one is born anew, he cannot see the kingdom of God (John 3:3). The word "anew" (*anothen*) could equally well be translated "from above" and the ambiguity is intentional.

The Prologue shows the Logos, "the only Son," (John 1:18), the bearer of life and light, become flesh and revealing the Father. So in the monologue which follows Nicodemus' withdrawal (John 3:11), Jesus speaks of the only Son descended from heaven to bring life and light to the world. This is why a rebirth is possible. "No one has ascended into heaven but he who descended from heaven, the Son of man" (John 3:13).

The incarnation of the Logos is the descent of the Son of Man, whom Daniel beheld on the clouds of heaven, into the realm of the flesh. And having descended from heaven the Son of Man can ascend again. His descent and ascent open to men the possibility of receiving eternal life, that is, of ascending to the sphere of spirit; in other words, the possibility of rebirth. The possibility becomes an actuality for those who have faith in the Son — which is tantamount (in terms of the Prologue) to "receiving the Logos," with the consequent power to be children of God. It is against this background that Jesus proclaims to Nicodemus: "As Moses lifted up the serpent in the wilderness, so must the Son of man be lifted up, that whoever believes in him may have eternal life" (John 3:14-15).

The first part of the verse recalls the episode of the bronze serpent reported in Numbers 21. While making their way around Edom the Israelites became impatient and spoke against God and against Moses. In punishment, "the Lord sent fiery serpents among the people," and many were bitten and died (Num. 21:6). After the people repented, the Lord said to Moses: "'Make a fiery serpent, and set it on a pole; and every one who is bitten, when he sees it, shall live.' So Moses made a bronze serpent, and set it on a pole; and if a serpent bit any man, he would look at the bronze serpent and live" (Num. 21:8-9).

The passage is assigned to the JE tradition. John Mauchline writes in *Hastings' Dictionary*: "Among many ancient peoples the serpent was regarded as sacred. The belief in its healing power was widespread (cf. especially the serpent of the Greek god of healing, Asklepios). Serpent figures have been found in Palestine in such circumstances as to indicate that they represented the *vis genetrix* in a context of fertility cults. The serpent symbol, *Nehustan*, in Jerusalem (2 Kings 18:4), which was destroyed by Hezekiah, may have been a pre-Davidic symbol which was taken over by the Israelites when they captured the city, or it may have been a well-known symbol in Palestine which they adopted for use in Yahweh worship. In either case the point of the story in Num. 21:4-9 was probably to show that healing comes from God and not from any magical properties inherent in the symbol."[21]

This interpretation is made explicit in the *Wisdom of Solomon*: "When the terrible rage of wild beasts came upon thy people . . . they received a token of deliverance to remind them of thy law's command. For he who turned toward it was saved, not by what he saw, but by thee, the Savior of all" (Wis. 16:5-6). This interpretation is found in the *Mishnah* as well: "But could the serpent slay or the serpent keep alive! — it is, rather, to teach thee that such time as the Israelites directed their thoughts on high and kept their hearts in subjection to their Father in heaven, they were healed; otherwise they pined away."[22]

Like "anew," the word "lift up" is a word of double meaning, and points both to exaltation in glory, and lifting up on the Cross. It is "one of those oscillating expressions of the fourth Evangelist embracing a profound paradox. It signifies both the going of Jesus to the Father (John 14:2) and his crucifixion (12:33)."[23] The thought runs as follows, says C. K. Barrett: "The Son of man is he who descends from heaven, and again ascends thither. Viewed in the conditions of his earthly life he is under necessity of being lifted up (exalted to glory); but his lifting up will be in the manner suggested by the serpent of the Old Testament. He will be lifted up on the cross (cf. especially 12:32f), and his lifting up will result not only in glory for himself but also in healing for mankind."[24]

---

[21] New York, 1963, 898.
[22] *Rosh ha-Shana* 318; Danby, *The Mishnah*, 192.
[23] Mauser, *op. cit.*, 75.
[24] *Op. cit.*, 178.

For John, Jesus' exaltation in glory and his being lifted upon the Cross are aspects of one and the same thing. In Mark the suffering and glorification are chronologically distinguished. In John one word is used to express both. And this is in accord with John's overall scheme, as we shall see later in John's use of another element of Exodus tradition, the Lamb of God. In John, Jesus dies at the very hour that the Passover lambs were being slain in the Temple. In John the Cross itself is the point of glorification, and cross, resurrection, and ascension form one vision of glorification.

"Though in John the cross must not be separated from the previous ministry," writes Professor Marsh, "it must not be separated on the other hand from the resurrection and ascension. And the resurrection narrative itself contains elements that are set out in temporal separation elsewhere. The ascension is clearly conceived as taking place on Easter Day. The gift of the Spirit and the Apostolic commission are related as taking place on the evening of Easter Day, and John ends his Gospel by repeating the simple but profound formula of a disciple's call: 'Follow me' (21:19). Thus John has told the Synoptic story so that neither docetism nor adoptionism can explain it, indeed so that only a Chalcedonian Christology is adequate; and he has told it so that nothing less than a Trinitarian theology will bear the weight of the good news that the Gospels contain."[25]

SIGN OF SALVATION

In his *Moses in the Fourth Gospel*, T. F. Glasson points out additional overtones to be found in this important Exodus passage. Thus from the Old Testament passage we see that the Lord's injunction was that the serpent should be made and raised up, "and everyone who is bitten, when he *sees* it, shall live." And so it proved to be. "If a serpent bit any man, he would *look at* the bronze serpent and live." The importance of beholding the Son is one of John's great themes. It is referred to throughout the Gospel and at its climax we find the words: "They shall look on him whom they have pierced" (John 19:37). The Old Testament passage links the ideas of seeing and living, over against which we

[25] Marsh, *op. cit.*, 763.

should set John 6:40, "This is the will of my Father, that every
one who sees the Son and believes in him should have eternal
life; and I will raise him up at the last day" (John 6:40). John
3:14 substitutes "believing" for "seeing," and this could well have
been with design. "In any case there is a close link between seeing and believing (cf. 20:8). In some cases there is the seeing of
the eyewitness; those who come later hear his testimony and believe. In this sense believing takes the place of seeing (cf. 19:35
and 20:29)" (Glasson, *op. cit.* 35). This kind of seeing is still
available to all through the Scriptures.

As we have already seen, the idea of Jesus' being lifted up is
central to the passage. In the Old Testament the term "lift up"
is often associated with a standard or ensign. The word used in
Numbers for the support to which the serpent was attached is the
word "standard" (Hebrew *nes*; LXX *semeion*). Isaiah speaks
several times of a standard or ensign being "lifted up" and *nasah*
is the verb he most often uses for this purpose. A standard is
raised, of course, to gather the dispersed. And here we come to
Jesus' saying in John 12:32, "I, when I am lifted up from the
earth, will draw all men to myself."

But the Hebrew word for standard (*nes*) can also mean miracle. In the LXX *nes* becomes *semeion*, which remarkably enough
can also mean both "sign" and "miracle." The center portion of
John's Gospel, of course, is a Book of Signs. But the greatest sign
of all is the sign of the Cross: the lifting up of the Son of Man in
suffering and glory. John has no miracle in his passion narrative.
Jesus' death and resurrection is the supreme sign.

And, finally, it is worth noting that the Brazen Serpent passage
(Num. 21) has traditionally been brought together with another
Exodus incident, Moses praying at Rephidim (Exod. 17:8-16).
On the way to Sinai, Israel is attacked by the Amalekites. Moses
tells Joshua to choose out men for the battle. Moses, accompanied
by Aaron and Hur, goes to stand on the top of the hill with the
rod of God in his hand. "Whenever Moses held up his hand, Israel
prevailed; and whenever he lowered his hand, Amalek prevailed.
But Moses' hands grew weary; so they took a stone and put it
under him, and he sat upon it, and Aaron and Hur held up his
hands, one on one side, and the other on the other side; so
his hands were steady until the going down of the sun. And

Joshua mowed down Amalek and his people with the edge of the sword" (Exod. 17:11-13).

This passage was brought together with the Brazen Serpent passage even in pre-Christian times; we find them together in Rabbinic writings. The Rephidim scene evokes the crucifixion so obviously that one wonders if John makes any allusion to it. And John does refer to the thieves on either side of the crucified Jesus in a way that differs from the Synoptics. The Synoptics say that Jesus was crucified with two *thieves*, one on the right hand, one on the left. John puts it this way: "Then they crucified him, and with him two others, one on either side, and Jesus between them (John 19:18). In Exodus 17, Aaron and Hur stand "one on one side, the other on the other side" (v. 12). A fairly obvious extension of the same association is found in Jesus' words to Peter: "When you are old, you will stretch out your hands, and another will gird you and carry you where you do not wish to go" (John 21:18). And John makes the application explicit in the parenthetical statement which follows: "(This he said to show by what death he was to glorify God)" v. 19.

JOHN 6 — BREAD OF LIFE

In John 6–8 we find three Exodus elements in Christian dress: the true bread, the living water, and the light of the world. It is highly significant that John mentions only seven of all the miracles Jesus performed and only one in common with all the Synoptics, the multiplication of the loaves (John 6). It is a good illustration of the degree to which John strives to bring out the significance of events rather than to merely relate them. It is also quite evident that John presupposes that his readers are acquainted with the Synoptic accounts of the incident.

C. H. Dodd suggests that a symmetry unites the incidents and the discourse of John 6. The sequence of incidents first shows Jesus feeding the five thousand. The result is that the people recognize Jesus as the Messiah and determine to make him king. Repudiating the multitude's mistaken notion of his messiahship, Jesus separates himself from the multitude, withdrawing to the hills. His disciples start across the lake in the dark and are overtaken by a storm. Jesus comes to them walking on the sea and identifies himself using the sacred name "I AM."

In the discourse also we find a progression from a false to a true conception of Jesus' messiahship. The multitude are prepared to see in Jesus a second Moses, who will restore the gift of manna. But Jesus is much more. He does not give a bread which perishes with the using but a bread which endures to eternal life. He is the true bread from heaven. Many disciples withdraw but Peter and the Twelve acknowledge that Jesus is the Holy One of God and that he has the words of eternal life.

John notes that the feeding of the multitude takes place when "the Passover, the feast of the Jews, was at hand" (John 6:4). There is no reason why this cannot be taken as a real chronological note, but beyond that, the Christian reader could hardly fail to remember that the Christian Passover was the Eucharist. Jesus' actions are the same as his actions at the Last Supper. In his commentary on St. Mark, D. E. Nineham writes: "Indeed to the early Christians the whole story would have been strongly reminiscent of their eucharistic worship, at which they too sat in orderly fashion while deacons brought round to them loaves blessed and broken by the celebrant. The story was interpreted as an anticipation of the Last Supper and the Eucharist. Often, no doubt, it will have been narrated when the little communities met to celebrate the Lord's Supper; how moving it must then have been, speaking, as it did, of one who would not let his followers perish in the 'desert' of this world but who could be relied on, not only for the necessities of this life, but for a supply of bread which is the pledge of (and the means of sustaining) survival into the kingdom of God. This last line of interpretation is, of course, fully and explicitly carried out by St. John (chapter 6); that fact, and the way he explicitly links the feeding with the gift of manna in the wilderness (vv. 31ff and 49f), may be held to justify the assumption that this interpretation was already leading that way in St. Mark's time, and so make plausible the fairly full exposition that has been derived from St. Mark's few hints."[26]

BREAD FROM HEAVEN

The essence of the miracle consisted in providing abundant food in the wilderness. But this is precisely what the Lord had done in the course of rescuing his people from Egypt by the

[26] *Op. cit.,* 179.

great act of salvation which was the basic foundation of Israel's history, and the central theme of its Law. Many passages of the Old Testament show how lively the remembrance of the manna in the desert remained. Psalm 78 recalls how the people tempted the Lord on that occasion. "They spoke against God, saying, 'Can God spread a table in the wilderness? He smote the rock so that water gushed out and streams overflowed. Can he also give bread, or provide meat for his people?'" (Ps. 78:19-20). The priest Ezra reminded the people how the Lord "gave them bread from heaven for their hunger and brought forth water for them from the rock for their thirst" (Neh. 9:15). The great prophet Elisha had performed a miracle which, though on a smaller scale, was strikingly like this one; through his servant he had distributed twenty barley loaves and a little fresh grain among one hundred men (2 Kings 4:42). "Thus Jesus' action was the 'fulfilment of the Law and the prophets'. It witnessed, though in a veiled fashion, to Jesus' Messiahship; he was the one sent by God to usher in the ultimate salvation to which Law and prophets had pointed forward."[27]

After the feeding of the five thousand, the people recognized Jesus as the Second Moses: "When the people saw the sign which he had done, they said, 'This is indeed the prophet who is to come into the world!'" (John 6:14). This is in accordance with the expectation that the Messiah, the second Deliverer, would repeat the signs of Moses, the first Deliverer. As a consequence the people seek by force to make Jesus king, which (as Dodd points out) is "a perfectly reasonable thing to do with a messiah" (*op. cit.* 345).

In the discourse which follows next day at Capharnaum, Jesus makes it clear that although the crowd had witnessed the multiplication of the loaves and had partaken of them, they had seen no further than food for the body which perishes with the using. They had not been nourished by "the food which endures to eternal life" (John 6:27). The crowd then demands that Jesus establish his messianic pretensions by restoring the gift of manna, assuming that this is what he meant by "food enduring to eternal life." Jesus answers with the insistence that the gift of manna in the wilderness came not from Moses but from God; indeed, the

[27] *Ibid.,* 178.

manna, however miraculous, was not the *true* bread from heaven which is now available in Jesus, who himself is the bread of life.

Then we should also bear in mind that bread is a standing symbol of the Torah. A further lesson would be implied. Moses did indeed give the Torah, of which manna is the symbol, but the "bread of Torah" is no more the knowledge of God "which endures to eternal life" than the manna is *true* bread. So Moses did not in the true sense give bread from heaven. This Jesus gives; this Jesus is. Moses (the Law) could not lead the people into Canaan; only Joshua (Jesus) could do that. It is the contrast that is emphasized, especially by John and the Epistle to the Hebrews.

The previous day Jesus showed himself to be a Giver of Bread. This can be kept within the limits of Jewish eschatological beliefs which conceived the Messiah as a Second Moses. But if Jesus is himself the food and drink of eternal life, we are well beyond merely messianic categories. The crowd is scandalized at Jesus' words and "after this many of the disciples drew back and no longer went about with him" (John 6:66). Only the Twelve remain faithful. In the Johannine equivalent to the confession at Caesarea Philippi, Peter exclaims: "Lord, to whom shall we go? You have the words of eternal life" (John 6:68).

JOHN 7 — LIVING WATER

Jesus as the True Bread (John 6) is followed by two other Exodus elements in Christian dress: the Living Water and the Rock (John 7), and the Light of the World (John 8). Actually the three chapters are closely interconnected. Manna and the water from the rock are closely connected in the historical context of the Exodus, and the same is true of water and light, both in the Exodus sources and later tradition, especially in the Feast of Tabernacles.

In chapter 6 the Feast of the Passover forms the background for the feeding of the multitude and Jesus' words on the true bread, clearly a preparation for the Eucharist, the Christian Passover. In chapters 7–8, it is the Feast of Tabernacles that ties the somewhat disparate material together and furnishes the background for the two principal symbols used: the living water, and the light of the world. At the beginning of chapter 7, "the Jews' feast of Tabernacles was at hand" (v. 2), and eventually Jesus goes up to Jerusalem for the feast, "not publicly but in private" (v. 10). The first discourse is given "about the middle of the feast" (John 7:14). Jesus' declaration about the living water is made "on the last day of the feast, the great day" (John 7:37). There is no indication of a change of scene until the end of chapter 8, where we read that "Jesus hid himself, and went out of the temple" (John 8:59).

At the end of a long evolution the Feast of Tabernacles also took on the character of an Exodus feast. When the Israelites came into the Promised Land they found the Canaanites observing a joyous autumnal feast after they had gathered the grapes from the vineyards, when they ate, drank, and reveled in the temple of their god, Baal (Judg. 9:27). "When the Jews were settled in Palestine and lived on the fruits of the earth, they also began the observance of this autumn festival. But, of course, they observed it in honor of their God, the God of Israel."[28]

THE AUTUMN FESTIVALS

The Israelites called this festival the Feast of Ingathering and it was celebrated in the seventh month (Tishri). It was observed for seven days and it began on the night of the September full-moon (the Harvest Moon). Marking as it did the end of one agricultural year, the Festival of the Ingathering was also a New Year festival. It is not surprising that the festival had the character of a revel, which the Israelites took over from the people about them. Nor is it surprising that their religious leaders found it unsuitable that the Chosen People should begin the new year with revelry just as their heathen neighbors did. They seem to have made efforts at a very early date to give the observance a more serious and religious mien.

Even in the time of Solomon's Temple, a definite day seems to have been established to cleanse the sanctuary of its profanations. "At the moment of the birth of the new year, its success must not be endangered by any of the preceding year's defilements; they must be swept away. Therefore the feast is often the occasion of a great temple cleaning and the burning of all that is soiled. Perhaps at times the purification was interior as well as exterior, that is, faults of cultic impurity contracted during the course of

28 H. Schauss, *The Jewish Festivals*, 171.

the old year were expiated." [29] When describing his ideal Temple, Ezekiel designated two days in the year to atone for sins committed against the sanctuary, one of which fell in the seventh month. Ezekiel here is not presenting something absolutely new, but seeking to reform an old custom.

The priests strove to convince the people that the autumn festival should either begin or end with a day of faith, expiation, and "reckoning of the soul." The Festival of Ingathering was fixed on the fifteenth Tishri and became the Feast of Booths or Tabernacles (Sukkoth); the new year observance was shifted to first Tishri and became the New Year feast (Rosh Hashonoh). But Rosh Hashonoh continued to display the effects of its association with the Day of Atonement, ushering in as it does a ten-day period of penance, which ends on Yom Kippur night.

Hastings' Dictionary summarizes the evolution as follows: "In pre-exilic times there was an autumnal feast, at the end of the Hebrew year, called the Feast of Ingathering. It was observed for seven days and it began on the night of the September full-moon (the Harvest Moon), Exod. 23:16; 34:22. In postexilic times this feast became broken up owing to the change of calendar. Part of the feast, the strictly new-year element, gravitated to the first of the seventh month (Tishri); part to the tenth of Tishri, becoming the Day of Atonement; while the rest kept to the night of the Harvest Full-Moon and became the Feast of Tabernacles." [30]

SEASONAL FEAST MADE HISTORICAL

In Deuteronomy, the name of the Feast of Ingathering is given as the Feast of Tabernacles or Booths: "You shall keep the feast of Booths seven days, when you make your ingathering from your threshing floor and your wine press" (Deut. 16:14). There seems to be little doubt but that this name arose from the use of booths of intertwined branches during the vintage. Theodor H. Gaster writes: "The booths were originally functional in character; they were simply the wattled cabins in which the harvesters and vintners were wont to lodge during the time of the ingathering. Such booths, made of plaited twigs of carob and oleander and roofed with palm leaves, are still used in the Holy Land through-

[29] T. Maertens, *A Feast in Honor of Yahweh*, 27.
[30] Pp. 951f.

out the period (from June to September) when the reaping is in progress, and it is in this sense that the word *succah* is usually employed in the Hebrew Bible."[31]

But Israel could not remain satisfied with the purely agricultural aspect of the festival. Like Passover and Pentecost, it too had to take on a historical as well as a seasonal significance. And the centralization of worship in Jerusalem undoubtedly had much to do with this. "The very fact that the provincial sanctuaries, the 'high places,' were abolished during Josiah's reign, and the Temple in Jerusalem was declared the only sanctuary for Jews, changed the character of Sukkos. The very appearance of the festival must have been different from the old days, now that all Jews made the pilgrimage to the one sanctuary in Jerusalem. The fact that all Jews were united in one place added a new national significance to the festival."[32]

And so the booths were made part of the Exodus tradition. "The traditional booths were interpreted as a reminder of those in which the ancestors of Israel had dwelt when they wandered through the wilderness on their journey from Egypt to the Promised Land! The festival thus became a logical sequel to Passover and Pentecost, which commemorated respectively the escape from bondage and the conclusion of the covenant at Sinai. Moreover, by themselves dwelling in booths at this season, each successive generation of Jews could be said to be sharing in that experience and thereby endowing it with a perpetual character."[33]

THE WATER CEREMONY

In Leviticus and Numbers elaborate ordinances are laid down for the observance of the feast, including a large number of offerings. In addition the *Mishnah* has preserved rites from the time of Herod's Temple. Two of these have especially strong overtones in John 7–8: a water ceremony, and a light ceremony. Both of these undoubtedly have their origin in the ancient agricultural Feast of the Ingathering. The feast marked the beginning of the winter rains (water ceremony) and coincided with the autumn equinox (light ceremony). Dodd observes that the water cere-

[31] *Festivals of the Jewish Year*, 81.
[32] Schauss, *op. cit.*, 174.
[33] Glazer, *op. cit.*, 84.

mony was "associated with prayers for rain, and may have been the survival of a primitive rain-making ceremony, since the festival was celebrated about the time when the first rains of autumn might be expected."[34]

The water ceremony is described in the *Mishnah* (Sukkah 4:19). This took place on each of the seven days of the Feast (and, according to inferior authorities) on the extra eighth day also. On other days of the year, after the burning of the daily sacrifice, a libation of wine was poured on the altar. But during Sukkos there was also a libation of water, with special ceremonies. Schauss gives the following sketch of the ceremony: "A merry throng gathers for the procession from the Mount of the Temple down to the spring of Shiloah. Leading the procession is a priest bearing a large golden ewer, in which he draws the water to be poured on the altar. He returns to the Temple and comes to the Water Gate which leads to the inner court. A great crowd awaits him there and greets him with joy. Priests carrying silver trumpets blow the ceremonial calls, . . . and other priests chant the words of the prophet, 'With joy shall ye draw water out of the wells of salvation' (Is. 12:3). At the same time another group of priests goes to Moza, a place near the city, to gather long willow branches which they place alongside the altar, with their points inward. The priest bearing the golden ewer of water marches into the inner court of the Temple, followed by the crowd, which joins the even greater assembly already in the court. The morning sacrifice has already been burned. The priest with the ewer proceeds to the altar, above which stand two containers made of silver, one for water and one for wine. Each of these containers has a narrow spout which is trained on the altar. The priest holds the ewer of water above the container and is about to pour. Many of the assembled multitude call out, asking him to raise his hand still higher, so that they can see that he is really pouring the water upon the altar, and not upon the ground."[35]

Hayyim Schauss points out in a note at this point that "we may assume that originally the water was poured upon the earth, as a talisman for rain, and only later, when it was made a part of the official ritual of the Temple, was it changed to a water-

[34] *Op. cit.*, 348f.
[35] *Op. cit.*, 181f.

offering for the altar."[36] In his *A Feast in Honor of Yahweh*, Dom Maertens follows up this older tradition. Tradition held that the bare rock of Mount Zion was visible in the temple ground and a legend soon explained that this was the rock that had accompanied the people during their desert trek and supplied them regularly with living water. Supposedly an echo of this legend is found in St. Paul's words to the Corinthians: "All ate the same supernatural food and drank the same supernatural drink. For they drank from the supernatural Rock which followed them, and the Rock was Christ" (1 Cor. 10:4). Maertens comments: "While water was being poured on the temple ground it was customary to read the account of the miracle of the rock of living water; in this way the historic fact was superimposed on the natural significance of fertility and the nomadic experience eclipsed the agrarian rite. Following this clue, many exegetes have wanted to find a spiritualization of the same kind in such secondary themes as the cloud, the mountain, etc."[37]

In any case, the water ceremony concludes as follows: "After the libation the priests with the trumpets again blow three calls, . . . and the ceremonial procession begins. Around the altar circles the long line of priests, bearing the willow branches. The Levites stand in choir formation and sing the Psalms of Praise. When they come to the words, 'We beseech Thee, O Lord, save now! We beseech Thee, O Lord, make us now to prosper!', the entire congregation gathered in the inner court raises the palm branches and twirls them in the air, joining the Levites and reciting in a great chorus: 'We beseech Thee, O Lord, save now! Were one looking down from above it would seem that not men but a forest of palm trees is shaking in the wind and asking the aid of God."[38]

RIVERS OF LIVING WATER

As we have noted above,[39] the Feast of Tabernacles forms the background of John 7–8. At the beginning of chapter 7, "The Jews' feast of Tabernacles was at hand" (v. 2), and eventually Jesus goes up to Jerusalem for the feast, "not publicly but in pri-

[36] *Ibid.*, 307, note 219.
[37] Maertens, *op. cit.*, 73.
[38] Schauss, *op. cit.*, 181f.
[39] *Supra*, 122.

vate" (John 7:10), and there is no indication of a change of scene until the end of chapter 8 where we read that "Jesus hid himself, and went out of the temple" (v. 59). Then, as Dodd observes, it is probable that the dialogues of chapter 7 themselves contain deliberate allusions to the water ceremony and the ideas associated with it. The most obvious of these appears in conjunction with an explicit reference to the feast. "On the last day of the feast, the great day, Jesus stood up and proclaimed, 'If any one thirst, let him come to me and drink. He who believes in me, as the Scripture has said, "Out of his heart shall flow rivers of living water."' Now this he said about the Spirit, which those who believed in him were to receive" (John 7:37-39).

In a succinct comment the *Oxford Annotated Bible* summarizes the wealth of meaning to be found in this passage. "For seven days water was carried in a golden pitcher from the Pool of Siloam to the temple as a reminder of the water from the rock in the desert (Num. 20:2-13), and as a symbol of hope for the coming Messianic deliverance (Is. 12:3). Jesus is the true water of life, who turns the symbol into reality (Is. 44:3; 55:1). Believers become channels of life to others, through Christ's *Spirit* given at Pentecost after he was *glorified* (crucified, risen, ascended). The gift of the *Spirit* was considered a mark of the Messianic age (Joel 2:28-29; Acts 2:14-21)."[40]

In John 6, bread is the central concept; in John 7 it is water. In the Old Testament and later writings, the manna and water from the rock are often linked. They go together as naturally as food and drink. John 6 presents Jesus as the bread corresponding to the manna. In John 7 we have the promise of living water set against the background of the Feast of Tabernacles which commemorated Israel's wilderness years. After declaring the fulfillment of the original gift of manna (6:31-35), John then declares the fulfillment of Moses' other great miracle. As Jesus is the Bread which came down from heaven and gives life to the world (John 6:33), so he is the rock from which the true water flows forth for the salvation of the world. It was in the same vein that Paul wrote to the Corinthians: "All ate the same supernatural food and all drank the same supernatural drink. For they drank from the supernatural Rock which followed them, and the Rock was Christ" (1 Cor. 10:3-4).

[40] *Op. cit.*, 1295f.

MESSIANIC TRANSFORMATION OF WILDERNESS

Another highly evocative circumstance is found in the fact
that Zechariah 14 was one of the traditional lections for the feast
of Tabernacles. Zechariah, whose prophecies date from 520 to
518, was a contemporary of Haggai. He shared the latter's zeal
for a rebuilt temple, but more elaborate prophecy appears in
Zechariah than in Haggai concerning the future age. In chapters
9—14 of the work, which constitute a Second Zechariah, the tone
becomes apocalyptic. Attention centers upon the woes and dis-
tresses which will usher in the final age when Jerusalem will become the center of a renewed land in a new age. Thus we read:
"On that day living waters shall flow out from Jerusalem, half
of them to the eastern sea and half of them to the western sea;
it shall continue in summer as in winter" (Zech. 14:8).

And the Feast of Tabernacles figures in this eschatological realization in a most striking way. "Then every one that survives of
all the nations that have come against Jerusalem shall go up year
after year to worship the King, the Lord of hosts, and to keep the
feast of booths. And if any of the families of the earth do not go
up to Jerusalem to worship the King, the Lord of hosts, there will
be no rain upon them. And if the family of Egypt do not go up
and present themselves, then upon them shall come the plague
with which the Lord afflicts the nations that do not go up to keep
the feast of booths. This shall be the punishment to Egypt and
the punishment to all the nations that do not go up to keep the
feast of booths" (Zech. 14:16-19).

As we saw earlier,[41] the Feast of Tabernacles was originally
a seasonal feast which under the influence of Israel's faith was
given an historical meaning. It was brought into conjunction with
Israel's wilderness years and the dwelling in tents. Here we see
the feast taking on a new, messianic and eschatological aspect.
Dom Maertens expresses this as a movement from history to
eschatology. After Israel settled in Palestine and became a nation, the Exodus memory began to fade. In times of persecution
a simple recalling of the past did not always seem relevant.

The prophetic movement imparted new interest by projecting
the Exodus concept into the not-too-distant future. Under these
circumstances, a feast like Tabernacles became not only com-

[41] *Supra,* 125.

memorative but also an expectation of similar experiences in the future. The feast looked mainly forward rather than backward; it was regarded eschatologically as anticipating the messianic era. Quite clearly this anticipation of the coming of the Kingdom of God, as the messianic age, is intimately connected with Tabernacles in Zechariah.

Second Isaiah also makes eschatological use of the Exodus theme, speaking of the messianic age as a transformation of the Wilderness. In Isaiah we read:

> I will open rivers on the bare heights,
>   and fountains in the midst of the valleys;
> I will make the wilderness a pool of water,
>   and the dry land springs of water.
> I will put in the wilderness the cedar,
>   the acacia, the myrtle, and the olive;
> I will set in the desert the cypress,
>   the plane and the pine together (Is. 41:18-19).

But by far the most vivid example of this eschatological usage is found in one of Ezekiel's visions, and the Tabernacle background appears certain. The last part of Ezekiel (cc. 33–48) is made up of oracles of hope, belonging after the fall of Jerusalem. To a helpless and hopeless people, Ezekiel brings hope of restoration to home and temple by their just and holy God. Ezekiel opens and closes with a vision of divine glory. The closing vision reaches its climax in a vision of the return of glory to the new Temple. The seer is brought to the door of the Temple and "behold, water was issuing from below the threshold of the temple toward the east (for the temple faced east); and the water was flowing down from below the south end of the threshold of the temple, south of the altar" (41:1).

The seer is led eastward and the stream of water becomes steadily deeper until it becomes a river. He is led back along the river and he sees that its banks are covered with trees and he is told: "This water flows toward the eastern region and goes down into the Arabah; and when it enters the stagnant waters of the sea, the water will become fresh. And wherever the river goes every living creature which swarms will live, and there will be very many fish; for this water goes there, that the waters of the sea may become fresh; so everything will live where the river goes. Fishermen will stand beside the sea; from En-gedi to En-eglaim it will be a place for the spreading of nets; its fish will be of very many kinds, like the fish of the Great Sea" (Ez. 41:8-10).

Second Isaiah foresees the time when the Lord will "open rivers on the bare heights"; Zechariah foretells that "on that day living waters shall flow out from Jerusalem"; Ezekiel beholds water "issuing below the threshold of the temple toward the east." The waters flow down the Brook Kidron and, becoming a river, work an eschatological transformation in the Wilderness. These messianic visions are associated with the Feast of Tabernacles and seem to have had their source in the water ceremony of that feast. In chapter 7, John shows Jesus proclaiming that "rivers of living water" would flow out of the believer's heart. And this took place "on the last day of the feast" of Tabernacles."[42]

As already noted, willow branches were placed alongside the altar for the water ceremony and the congregation carried palm branches, so that "were one looking down from above it would seem that not men but a forest of palm trees is shaking in the wind and asking the aid of God."[43]

This ceremony seems to be reflected in Ezekiel's vision of messianic fertility produced by the river flowing from the Temple. He writes: "On the banks, on both sides of the river, there will grow all kinds of trees for food. Their leaves will not wither nor their fruit fail, but they will bear fresh fruit every month, because the water for them flows from the sanctuary. Their fruit will be for food, and their leaves for healing" (47:12).

And for his part, Zechariah associates the living water with the universal recognition of Yahweh's kingship. He writes: "Everyone that survives of all the nations that have come against Jerusalem shall go up year after year to worship the King, the Lord of hosts, and to keep the feast of booths" (Zech. 14:16). Dom Maertens points out that "the feast of the seventh month, like the feast of the New Year, since pagan days, had been a feast of the enthronement of a god. Now the living water, showered upon all the nations in the form of graces, will ensure the kingship of Yahweh who is enthroned over the whole universe."[44]

[42] *Supra*, 122.
[43] Schauss, *op. cit.*, 182.
[44] *Op. cit.*, 77f.

WATER FROM JESUS' SIDE

The most obvious reference in John 7 to the Tabernacles background, then, is found in Jesus' declaration, "on the last day of the feast," when he stood up and declared: "If any one thirst, let him come to me and drink. He who believes in me, as the Scripture has said, 'Out of his heart shall flow rivers of living water'" (John 7:37-38). There is a long-standing discussion about the punctuation of these verses. The alternate reading in the RSV gives the other possibility: "If any one thirst, let him come to me, and let him who believes in me drink. As the Scripture has said, 'Out of his heart shall flow rivers of living water.'"

One result of this punctuation is that v. 38 may be taken as a reference to Jesus and not to the believer. This latter reading does take on rich meaning viewed against the Tabernacles background and its water ceremony. An Exodus feast, Tabernacles recalled the rock smitten in the wilderness from which water flowed. The Zechariah lection speaks of living water flowing out from Jerusalem; St. Paul speaks of the Israelites' drinking of the supernatural rock which is Christ. This reading also points forward to Jesus' passion when, as John records: "One of the soldiers pierced his side with a spear, and at once there came out blood and water" (John 19:36).

C. K. Barrett writes concerning this verse: "It is . . . probable that John saw in what he narrated primarily as a historical fact a second meaning. Water and blood are significant words in this Gospel; see especially 3:5; 4:14; 6:53ff; 7:37f; 13:5; cf. 1 John 5:6, 8. Christ is the dispenser of the water and blood by which men are regenerated and live, and these issue precisely from his death, which is the means by which salvation and eternal life are achieved. It is, further, true that water and blood suggest baptism and the Eucharist respectively; these sacraments find their meaning only in the death which is the life of men." [45]

Moreover, a number of commentators point to a Jewish tradition that when Moses struck the rock, it first gushed out blood and then water.[46] This would strengthen the type-antitype relationship and would be a further indication that Jesus is truly the true blood of the New Covenant.

[45] *Peake's Commentary on the Bible*, 866.
[46] Glasson, *op. cit.*, 54.

JOHN 8 — THE LIGHT CEREMONY

Another Feast of Tabernacles ceremony described in the *Mishnah* is *Beth ha-She'ubah*, a fire-observance with a torch dance (Sukkah 5:1-4). It seems a likely conjecture that the observance was originally connected in some way with the autumnal equinox (about September 26). The ceremony took place at night in the Court of the Women. Schauss describes it as follows: "Above, on the roof of the colonnades that encircle the court, galleries have been built for the women; below them are the men. In the center of the court burn great golden menorahs, set on bases that are fifty yards high. Each menorah has four branches, which terminate in huge cups into which oil is poured. Four ladders are placed against each menorah and four young priests mount them and pour oil into the cups to keep the wicks burning. (The wicks were made from the worn-out garments of the priests.) The light of these menorahs attains such intensity that all Jerualem is lit up by them."[47]

Theodor Gaster adds the following: "Men of piety and good works danced in front of them, waving burning torches, while a throng of Levites, standing on the fifteen steps which divided the Court of the Women from that of the Israelites, furnished accompanying music. At the Nicanor Gate stood priests, holding trumpets. At cockcrow, they ascended the steps and sounded a series of prolonged and quavering blasts. When they reached the gate which leads out to the east, they turned their faces westward, in the direction of the Temple building, and cried: 'Our forefathers, when they were in this place, turned their backs to the Temple of the Lord and their faces toward the rising sun in the east (cf. Ez. 8:16), but we — our eyes are turned toward the Lord.'"[48]

All the elements of the autumn festival had to take on an Exodus meaning. The vintage booths were associated with the tents of the wilderness years. The water ceremony was associated with the water from the rock and the light ceremony was associated with the pillar of fire.

In John 6 Jesus speaks of the true bread in conjunction with the Feast of Passover. In John 7–8, Jesus speaks of water and

[47] *Op. cit.*, 183.
[48] *Op. cit.*, 82f.

light in conjunction with the Feast of Booths. "On the last day of the feast, the great day, Jesus stood up and proclaimed, 'If any one thirst, let him come to me, and let him who believes in me drink. As the Scripture has said, "Out of his heart shall flow rivers of living water"'" (John 7:37-38). And in chapter 8 we read: "Again Jesus spoke to them, saying, 'I am the light of the world; he who follows me will not walk in darkness, but will have the light of life'" (v. 12).

THE LIGHT OF THE WORLD

As we saw above, Jesus goes up to Jerusalem for the Feast of Tabernacles, "not publicly but in private" (John 7:10), and Jesus' discourse on the living water is made on the last day of the feast, the great day (v. 37). But there is no indication of a change of scene until the end of chapter 8 where we read that "Jesus hid himself and went out of the temple" (v. 59). Therefore the dialogues of chapter 8 are also to be viewed against the background of the Feast of Tabernacles.

The fifth dialogue in the series (Dodd's Fourth Episode) begins with Jesus' declaration: "I am the light of the world; he who follows me will not walk in darkness, but will have the light of life." At the end of the dialogue it is recorded that "these words he spoke in the treasury, as he taught in the temple" (John 8:20). Just as we found a solid line of meaning connecting Jesus the Living Water, the water ceremony of the Feast of Booths, and the water from the rock in the desert, so here we can see a line of meaning running through Jesus the Light of the World, the light ceremony of the feast, and the pillar of fire in the desert. Jesus is the eschatological realization of the pillar of fire in the desert and all that it represents, and those who follow him will have the light of life.

Mention of the treasury (John 8:20) is another link with the light ritual, since the treasury was adjacent to the women's court, where the ceremony took place. And in the reading from Zechariah 14 there were eschatological references to light as well as water; verse 7 reads: "On that day . . . there shall be continuous day (it is known to the Lord), not day and not night, for at evening time there shall be light." Professor Ackroyd comments on this verse: "The new age will see the end of the present seasonal divisions (cf. Gen. 8:22), and of day and night; water will be abundant all the year round (7f). The bracketed phrase in 7 may be a pious comment: 'God only knows when this new age will dawn'—or possibly it means '(continuous day) is known to God'—he dwells in eternal light (cf. Is. 60:19f)."[49]

As we noted above,[50] bread (chapter 6) and water (chapter 7) were often linked together in the Old Testament and later writings. The passages cited also contain references to the pillar of fire (Ps. 105:39-41; Neh. 9:12, 15). In later tradition the three gifts (manna, pillar of fire, and water) were associated with Moses, Miriam and Aaron respectively. When Miriam died the well was taken away, when Aaron died the cloud of glory was taken away, when Moses died the manna ceased. In John 6, 7, 8 we have the Christian fulfillment of the three great wilderness gifts (bread, water, fire).

THE SHEKINAH

Nor is that an end to the ideas that would be evoked by the Feast of Tabernacles (Sukkos) which forms a background to John 6–7. Suggesting the idea of the Lord's eschatological tenting with his people, it is a subtle affirmation of the Incarnation.

As with most themes in John's Gospel, this thread of ideas is anticipated in the Prologue. John 1:14 reads: "And the Word became flesh and dwelt among us, full of grace and truth; we have beheld his glory, glory as of the only Son from the Father." The key words here are "dwelt" and "glory" and much of St. John's thought rests upon a play on these words in their Greek and Hebrew forms. In some translations "dwelt among us" is rendered "tabernacled among us," which makes the reference to the Tabernacle evident.

The Greek word for "dwell" is *skēnoō* and the Greek word for "tabernacle" is *skēnē*. Moreover the thread of thought runs back into the Hebrew. John 1:14 recalls the Lord's words to Moses: "Let them make me a sanctuary, that I may dwell in their midst" (Exod. 25:8). The Hebrew word for "dwell" here is *shaken*. *Mishkān* ("dwelling place"), from the same root, is the term used to designate the tent in the Jerusalem tradition. *Shaken* in turn lies

49 *Peake's Commentary,* 655.
50 *Supra,* 128.

at the root of *Shekinah*, to which so much meaning is attached, and Glory and Shekinah are intimately associated.

In its earlier stages, the Old Testament used anthropomorphisms quite freely. God was spoken of in human terms; he was said to dwell in a certain place and to be seen, and the like. Later thought objected to this usage, regarding it as a dangerous materializing of the divine nature. Various devices were adopted to prevent popular misunderstanding. In the Targums, the Aramaic paraphrases which had come into use by Jesus' time, substitutes for the Divine Name were used: Word (*mēmrā*), Spirit, Wisdom.

One of the most important of these was Shekinah, which designated God's dwelling, God's presence, among his people. Thus in the Targums the phrase "God dwells" becomes "the Shekinah rests"; God's hiding his face is the removal of the Shekinah. Now God's presence was often manifested by a fiery appearance, or a light in a cloud. Such manifestation is the Glory. The principal Hebrew word for "glory" is *kābhōdh*, which is derived from the verbal root *kābhēdh*, meaning "to be heavy." It acquires other meanings such as wealth or abundance, esteem, dignity, prestige, honor, and splendor. The Kabod or Glory is not God, but an effluence from him, or from his Shekinah. The Shekinah is the source and center of the Glory.

The Shekinah had manifested itself on Sinai and in the wilderness; it had dwelt in the Tabernacle and in the Temple. After the destruction of Jerusalem, the people were torn between the conviction that the Shekinah was inseparable from Israel, and the fear that it had withdrawn because of the sins of the people.

In his vision of Jerusalem's destruction, Ezekiel saw the "glory of the Lord" leave the city. "The glory of the Lord went forth from the threshold of the house, and stood over the cherubim. And the cherubim lifted up their wings and mounted up from the earth in my sight as they went forth, with the wheels beside them; and they stood at the door of the east gate of the house of the Lord; and the glory of the God of Israel was over them. . . . And the glory of the Lord went up from the midst of the city, and stood upon the mountain which is on the east side of the city" (Ez. 10:19; 11:23).

A Rabbinic tradition relates that the Shekinah tarried on the Mount of Olives for three and a half years in the hope that Israel would repent, but they did not (Midrash Rabba on Lam. 82).

In the end of time, in the eschatological age, the great saving acts of the past will be repeated and then, of course, the Shekinah will again dwell among his people Israel. Ezekiel ends his description of restored Jerusalem with the declaration: "The name of the city henceforth shall be, The Lord is there" (48:35). In an oracle of restoration, Isaiah declares that when Israel has been cleansed, "then the Lord will create over the whole site of Mount Zion and over her assemblies a cloud by day, and smoke and the shining of a flaming fire by night; for over all the glory there will be a canopy and a pavilion" (Is. 4:5).

The Second Book of Maccabees relates that when Jeremiah left Jerusalem before its destruction, he ordered that the tent and the ark should follow with him, and he went out to the mountain where Moses had gone up and had seen the inheritance of God. And Jeremiah came and found a cave, and he brought there the tent and the ark and the altar of incense, and he sealed up the entrance. Some of those who followed him came up to mark the way, but could not find it. When Jeremiah learned of it, he rebuked them and declared: "The place shall be unknown until God gathers his people together again and shows his mercy. And then the Lord will disclose these things, and the glory of the Lord and the cloud will appear" (2:4-8).

THE ESCHATOLOGICAL TENTING

In 1:14 John writes: "The Word became flesh and dwelt among us . . . and we saw his glory." Here the expressions "glory" and "dwell" are combined and the latter (*skēnoō* in Greek) was probably intentionally chosen to represent Skekinah. God's personal presence in Christ is connected with his earlier presence in the Tabernacle. What was formerly symbol is now manifest "in flesh"; the vagueness of the Jewish conception gives place to the definite presence of the personal Christ.

This understanding of John 1:14 lends greater depth to a number of other New Testament texts. Thus the angel of the Lord appeared to the shepherds in the field and "the glory of the Lord shone around them" (Luke 2:9). In the Transfiguration "a bright cloud" overshadows Jesus, Moses, and Elijah (Matthew 17:5).

In 1 Peter we read: "If you are reproached for the name of

Christ, you are blessed, because the spirit of glory and of God rests upon you" (4:14). The glory rests upon Christ as it rested upon the Tabernacle and in turn it rests upon the members of his Body in the moment of special identification. The letter to the Hebrews declares that in these last days God has spoken through a Son who "reflects the glory of God and bears the very stamp of his nature" (Heb. 1:3). And in James, Jesus is called Shekinah: "Hold the faith of our Lord Jesus Christ, the Lord of glory" (James 2:11).

John's writing that the Word "dwelt among us" recalls how God was present in the midst of Israel in the wilderness period and after. The Shekinah was made manifest by the cloud which was associated with both the Tabernacle and the Temple. Now the Shekinah dwells among God's new people because the Word has become flesh in Jesus and men can behold the Glory in him.

The dwelling in tents or booths (*sukkoth*) was a prominent feature of the wilderness days and later became the characteristic feature of the Feast of Tabernacles. John 7—8 unfolds against the background of the Feast of Tabernacles, effectively evoking all these associations and indicating the realization of the eschatological aspects of the Feast of Tabernacles in the person of Jesus.

Jesus' body is the final tabernacle wherein the Shekinah, the Glory, will dwell definitively. It is with good reason then that Christian thought has found a close link between the Feast of Tabernacles and the Incarnation. As the Passover is a type of Christ's passion, and Pentecost a type of the sending of the Holy Spirit, so the Feast of Tabernacles is a type of the Incarnation: the Word's becoming flesh and dwelling among men.

We noted earlier[51] that there are strong reasons for believing that the *logos* doctrine in John found its origin in Hebrew Wisdom. When John wrote of the Logos' dwelling among men, he probably had the book of Sirach in mind as well as the book of Exodus. In Sirach, Wisdom personified declares: "The Creator of all things gave me a commandment, and the one who created me assigned a place for my tent. And he said, 'Make your dwelling (*kataskēnoō*) in Jacob, and in Israel receive your inheritance'" (24:8.)

This passage in Sirach comes from a sustained hymn of praise

[51] *Supra*, 109.

of wisdom in which wisdom is clearly identified with the Torah. As Glasson points out, "it is likely that the Prologue's main interest is to show how Christ takes the place of the Torah; all that had been claimed for the latter is here ascribed to the Logos-Son of God" (*op. cit.* 66).

When John writes that the Word "dwelt among us," he is affirming that the Tabernacle of God is again with men and that the eschatological Glory is present in Jesus. It is significant that Jesus spoke of the Temple and his body in the same breath. When the Jews asked for a sign, Jesus answered: "Destroy this temple, and in three days I will raise it up." And John explains: "He spoke of the temple of his body" (John 2:19, 21). And as at times the Glory could not be confined to the Tabernacle or Temple, so in the earthly life of Jesus the Glory within him was at times manifested outwardly. But in this respect there is a notable difference between the Synoptics and St. John. The Synoptics recount the Transfiguration; St. John is interested in showing that Jesus' entire life is a manifestation of the Glory.

VISION OF HEAVEN OPENED

We saw earlier that the Transfiguration has strong Exodus elements. Moses and Elijah, wilderness prophets, were the most prominent among those prophets expected to return in the end time. Just as Moses' face shone when he came down from the mountain, "because he had been talking with God" (Exod. 24:39), so in the Transfiguration, Jesus' face "shone like the sun, and his garments became white as light," and, later, "a bright cloud overshadowed them" (Matthew 17:2, 5). Probably one of the purposes of the Transfiguration account is to show that Jesus' splendor exceeded that of Moses because he enjoyed an even closer connection with God. And Peter's desire to build three booths seems to follow from his impression that the full eschatological realization of the Feast of Tabernacles, the Lord's ultimate dwelling with his people, had now arrived.

Already in the Prologue, John draws a sharp contrast between Moses and Jesus: "The Law was given through Moses; grace and truth came through Jesus Christ" (1:17). And John continues: "No one has ever seen God; the only Son, who is in the bosom of the Father, he has made him known" (1:18). This seems to

allude to the Exodus declaration that man cannot see God and
live (Exod. 33:22), and clearly expresses Jesus' superiority over
Moses.

Several other New Testament passages stress the same point.
Thus the Epistle to the Hebrews declares that "Jesus was counted
worthy of as much more glory than Moses as the builder of a
house has more honor than the house" (Heb. 3:3). And dealing
specifically with Exodus 34, St. Paul writes to the Corinthians:
"Now if the dispensation of death, carved in letters on stone,
came with such splendor that the Israelites could not look at
Moses' face because of its brightness, fading as this was, why
should not the dispensation of the Spirit be attended with greater
splendor?" (2 Cor. 3:7-8).

Paul then proceeds to make a daring application to Christ's
members. For the Jew the veil remains in place; "through Christ
is it taken away. Yes, to this day whenever Moses is read a veil
lies over their minds; but when a man turns to the Lord the
veil is removed. Now the Lord is the Spirit, and where the Spirit
of the Lord is, there is freedom. And we all, with unveiled face,
beholding the glory of the Lord, are being changed into his likeness from one degree of glory to another; for this comes from
the Lord who is the Spirit" (2 Cor. 3:14-16).

As we saw earlier,[52] John brings his first chapter to a climax
with Jesus' words to Nathanael: "Truly, truly I say to you, you
will see heaven opened, and the angels of God ascending and
descending upon the Son of man" (1:51). In Dodd's view, all the
rest of John's Gospel is controlled by this revelation of the Son of
Man. "The whole series of 'signs' which follows, culminating in
the supreme sign of the cross and resurrection, *is* the vision of
the heaven opened and the angels of God ascending and descending upon the Son of Man. And these 'signs' are history. 'The Logos was made *flesh* – and we beheld His glory'" (*op. cit.* 294).

The Synoptics indicate that the Transfiguration takes place
"after six days" (Luke: "eight days"). This has definite Exodus
overtones. Exodus 24:16 records: "The glory of the Lord settled
on Mount Sinai, and the cloud covered it six days; and on the
seventh day he called to Moses out of the midst of the cloud."
So at the beginning, in the middle, and at the climax of John's
Gospel, we note periods of six days followed by a manifestation of

[52] *Supra*, 108.

Jesus' glory on the seventh. John relates incidents on four successive days and John 2 begins: "On the third day there was a marriage at Cana." After relating the incident, John observes: "This, the first of his signs, Jesus did at Cana in Galilee, and manifested his glory" (v. 11).

Then in John 7, the week of the Feast of Tabernacles is the unifying background. Here again it is after six days that Jesus manifests himself with the declaration: "I am the light of the world" (8:12). Again, at the beginning of the passion narrative, John writes: "Six days before the Passover, Jesus came to Bethany" (12:1). In John, of course, Jesus dies on the Passover (a notable departure from Synoptic tradition). Thus it is brought out in a most striking manner that Jesus' being lifted up on the Cross is the crowning glory of all, and again this came on the seventh day. This is underlined by the fact that John does all that he can to keep the exaltation of the Cross, from the grave, and into heaven as a single movement.

THE NAME OF THE LORD

Finally, in John 7–8, the Tabernacles chapters, there are possible allusions, allusions of the greatest subtlety, to another Exodus element. This would involve allusions to a special form of the Lord's sacred name in these chapters and this would have to be viewed as part of a pattern of meaningful allusions to the sacred name in John in general.

In 8:24 we hear Jesus declare: "You will die in your sin unless you believe that I am he." "I am he" (in Greek, *Ego eimi*) translates a Hebrew phrase (*Ani-hu*) which is another form of the sacred name (YHWH) revealed to Moses in the vision of the burning bush. Again in 8:28 we hear Jesus say: "When you have lifted up the Son of man, then you will know that *I am he* (*Ego eimi=Ani-hu*).

But then in 8:16 we seem to have an allusion to a special form of the Lord's sacred name. There we hear Jesus declare: "Yet even if I do judge, my judgment is true, for it is not I alone that judge, but *I and he* who sent me." In the phrase "I and he," the usual *Ego eimi* has become *Ego kai ho* and when we trace this back to the Hebrew it would mean that the usual *Ani-hu* would become *Ani-w^{e}hu*, with the addition of the conjunction "and" (wᵉ) between *Ani* and *hu*. This becomes significant when it is seen in conjunction with something found in the *Mishnah*.

The second division of the *Mishnah* (Moed), which deals with "Set Feasts," records various traditions concerning the celebration of the Feast of Tabernacles. It is recorded that the celebrants went to a place in Jerusalem called Motza and there cut themselves young willow-branches. Then "they came and set these up at the sides of the Altar so that their tops were bent over the Altar. They then blew [on the *shofar*] a sustained, a quavering and another sustained blast. Each day they went in procession a single time around the altar, saying, *Save now, we beseech thee, O Lord! We beseech thee, O Lord, send now prosperity*. R. Judah says: '*Ani waho*! save us we pray.' *Ani waho*! save us we pray!'" (Sukkah 4:5; Danby 178).

The petition is from Psalm 118:25. However, Rabbi Judah ben Ilai (c. A.D. 130–60), one of the Rabbis most often quoted in the *Mishnah*, indicates that a special form of the sacred name was used, *Ani waho*. And Danby writes in the footnote: "Instead of the repeated 'We beseech thee, O Lord (*ana* YHWH, which includes pronouncing the Sacred Name), they modify the sounds to *ani waho*."

As is well known, a name was more than a label for the ancient Semites. What a person was, his personality or essence, was involved with and expressed by his name. To know a person's name was to know the person himself. "To know the name" of God sums up the ideal attitude of the Israelite to his God. "To proclaim his name" was the vocation of the servant of God. Dodd writes: "The name of a person is the symbol of his personal identity, his status, and his character; and so, for the Hebrew monotheist, the Name of God stands as a symbol for His sole deity, His glory, and His character as righteous and holy" (*op. cit.* 93).

SHEM HAMMEPHORASH

In the course of time the Chosen People gave up pronouncing the sacred name (YHWH) which was connected with the vision of the burning bush. The actual name as distinctly pronounced came to be called the *shem hammephorash* and it began to figure in the eschatological expectation. When the Age to Come arrived, many of the events of the Exodus period would be repeated, indeed, some of the Exodus personages would reappear. In the age of realization, the *shem hammephorash* will also come into use again.

There are a number of passages in Second Isaiah where *Ani-hu* figures prominently. And when these passages were translated into Greek, the Septuagint translators treated *Ani-hu* as a proper name. Thus in Isaiah 43:25 we read:

> I, I am He
> who blots out your transgressions for my own sake
> and I will not remember your sins.

The verse would therefore begin, "I, *Ani-hu*, who blot out your transgressions." Or in the Septuagint, "I, *Ego Eimi*, who blot out your transgressions." And in 45:18 we read: "Thus says the Lord . . . 'I am the Lord, there is no other!'" In the Septuagint LORD (ʏʜᴡʜ) is translated *Ego Eimi*. In the following verse we read: "I the LORD speak the truth." Here the Septuagint translators seem to have translated the word LORD (ʏʜᴡʜ) twice, once by *Ego Eimi* and once by *Kyrios*, giving, "I am *Ego Eimi*, the *Kyrios*, who speaks the truth." In Second Isaiah there are even hints of the belief that the *shem hammephorash* will be used again in the age to come. In Isaiah 52:6, for example, we hear the Lord declare: "Therefore my people shall know my name; therefore in that day they shall know that it is I who speak (they shall know that *Ani-hu* [*Ego Eimi*] is speaking): 'Here am I.'" Here *Ani-hu* (*Ego Eimi*) is treated as the name of God (the *shem hammephorash*) which shall be revealed in the age to come.

On the other hand, it would seem that the Rabbis found the special form of *Ani-hu, Ani-weʰhu*, in the Old Testament only with the aid of some rehandling. Thus quoting Rabbi Judah, the *Mishnah* records a tradition that it was used in quoting Ps. 118 on the Feast of Tabernacles, as we have seen. And elsewhere in Rabbinic literature it is seen that special significance was attached to the form *Ani-weʰhu*. It was taken to stand for the intimate association, or quasi-identification of God and his people. Thus Ps. 80:3 reads: "Stir up thy might and come save us." Commenting on this verse, Rabbi Abbahu, with a slight emendation (*leʰkāh*, "come," is read as *leká*, "thyself"), makes it read: "Stir up thy might and come save thyself," with the idea that in rescuing Israel, God rescues himself. The same Rabbi takes the *Ani-wehu* of the Feast of Tabernacles to be a prayer that God would help his people and himself.

Similarly, 2 Sam. 7:23 declares that the Lord redeemed the people Israel "for himself" from Egypt. Rabbi Aqiba makes "himself" a direct object, giving the sense that the Lord had saved himself out of Egypt. Indeed, it may be that one variant of this kind won a place in the canonical text. In Isaiah 63:9 the RSV has: "In all their affliction he was afflicted," while a footnote reads: "Another reading is *he did not afflict*." In this instance "he" (*lō*) is read for "not" (*lo'*).

While, on the one hand, the name *Ani-wehu* signifies the solidarity of God with his people in their troubles, on the other hand, it also implies the duty of Israel to become like God. Exodus 15:2 reads: "This is my God and I will praise him." In Hebrew the consonants for "I will praise him" are the same as those for *Ani-wehu*. Understood in this sense the verse would read: "This is my God, I and he." Rabbi Abba Shaul understands it in this sense and comments: "Let us be like God; as He is merciful and gracious, so be thou merciful and gracious," implying a community of character between God and Israel, as elsewhere there is community of suffering.[53]

Admittedly, we moderns find this extremely subtle but it is no more subtle than many parts of the New Testament. And, as C. H. Dodd points out: "The doctrine of the solidarity of God with His people is implicit in much of the Old Testament, and its explicit statement goes back at least to Aqiba. There seems no reason to reject R. Judah ben Ilai's statement that the form *Ani-wehu* was actually employed by the priests in the temple (i.e., before A.D. 70). It is not impossible that the traditional interpretation of it may have had its beginnings during the period to which the Fourth Gospel belongs, and that the evangelist may have been aware of the profound idea that the Name of God can be known (that is, His true character can be apprehended) only where His intimate unity with His people is appreciated."[54]

[53] Cf. Dodd, *op. cit.*, 95.
[54] *Ibid.*, 95.

THE MULTITUDE AND THE DISCIPLES

There are some subtle indications that John also uses the doctrine of the name to evoke the Exodus theme. One instance is found in the Bread of Life passage (chapter 6, Dodd's Third Episode), which is set against the background of the Feast of the Passover. Jesus crosses the Sea of Galilee and the multitude followed him. Jesus went up into the hills, and "the Passover, the feast of the Jews, was at hand" (John 6:4). The narrative of the feeding of the five thousand is substantially the same as the Synoptic versions. As happens in other instances (at Jacob's well, chapter 4; in the Temple on the Feast of Tabernacles, chapter 7), Jesus' sign leads those who witnessed it to recognize him as the coming Prophet. John 6:14 reads: "When the people saw the sign which he had done, they said, 'This is indeed the prophet who is to come into the world!'"

Perceiving that the people would make him king, Jesus withdraws to the hills while his disciples row away across the lake. Darkness fell and a storm arose and then Jesus comes to them walking on the sea and he pronounces the sacred formula: I AM (*Ani-hu, Ego Eimi*). Jesus "said to them, 'It is I; do not be afraid!'" (John 6:20).

It may well be that John got this sequence of events from tradition, but, as Dodd says, John's temporal sequences seem nearly always to be more than merely temporal. John seeks for the deeper meaning. And a subtle parallel does seem to unite the preliminary incidents (feeding of the multitude, attempt to make Jesus king, and walking on the sea) and the discourse which follows (6:25-71). As in other episodes, the discourse indicates a progression from a false or inadequate conception of Jesus' status and mission to a more adequate one.

After seeing the sign, the people are prepared to see in Jesus a second Moses who will restore the gift of manna. Many expected a repetition of this Exodus element at the opening of the messianic age. But this is not enough. Manna is not true bread from heaven. Indeed, he is the true bread from heaven. Further, bread is a symbol of Torah. Moses gave manna (Torah), but Jesus gives the true bread (knowledge of God that is everlasting life). Faced with this circumstance, men must choose for or against. Those who are unable to take the required step are separated from those who, in some measure at least, are willing to take it. The multitude is scandalized, and even "many of his disciples drew back and no longer went about with him" (John 6:66). The twelve confess that Jesus is the Holy One of God, he who has the words of eternal life.

It appears, then, that we have a similar progression in the incidents and the dialogue. After the feeding, the multitude recognize Jesus as "the prophet who is to come," as the Messiah. Consequently the multitude seek by force to make Jesus king. Jesus withdraws and then proceeds to separate his own men from the multitude, dismissing the latter from his entourage. The disciples too are temporarily separated and in the dark. "But almost immediately they receive enlightenment. Christ appears to them 'upon the waters', and He pronounces the sacred formula: EGO EIMI. It is true that in the story, taken at its face value, these words might mean, as they do in the Synoptic parallels, no more than 'It is I'; but in view of the importance which the formula bears in other Johannine passages it seems more than probable that it is to be understood here as elsewhere as the equivalent of the divine name ANI-HU, I AM. It appears, therefore, that the sequence of incidents gives a progression parallel to that which we find in the discourse. If so, then the narrative of the Feeding of the Multitude is not only significant or symbolical in itself, but it constitutes, in conjunction with the two incidents following, a complex *semeion* which is elucidated, after the Johannine manner, in the appended discourse."[55]

And how meaningful it is to note that in the light of a great many Old Testament texts, Jesus' "walking upon the sea" possesses an Exodus meaning in itself. Speaking of the Lord's manifestation in the thunderstorm, Ps. 29:3 declares: "The voice of the Lord is upon the waters; the God of glory thunders, the Lord, upon many waters." Inevitably the Israelite would think also of the Lord's dividing the waters of the Red Sea in the exodus from Egypt. And Ps. 77 makes this explicit: "Thy way was through the sea, thy path through the great waters; yet thy footprints were unseen" (v. 19).

[55] *Ibid.*, 344f.

ANI-WᵉHU: GOD AND ISRAEL

The next group of signs (Dodd's Fourth Episode) is set against the background of the Feast of Tabernacles. Jesus delivers a number of discourses on the last day of the feast. He declares that he is the light of the world (which we have connected with the light ceremony of the Feast of Tabernacles). Some signs of tradition point to the use of *Ani-wᵉhu* on the Feast of Tabernacles.[56] And there seems to be a reflection of this in the very next discourse (8:21-30). Jesus tells the Jews: "I told you that you would die in your sins, for you will die in your sins unless you believe that I am he" (John 8:24). And again: "When you have lifted up the Son of man, then you will know that I am he" (John 8:28).

Ani-wᵉhu was interpreted to imply the intimate union of God with Israel. It is implied that the inmost nature of God can be expressed only in a name which declares that "I and he," God and Israel, are in union. So here, "that I am he," (*hoti* EGO EIMI) reflects the Old Testament usage of the divine name. It appears again in v. 28, and is followed by the declaration: "He who sent me is with me" (John 8:29). In 8:16 also we have the phrase "I and he who sent me." These recall even verbally the formula *Ani-wᵉhu*, "and the meaning attributed to it in rabbinic tradition, Christ taking the place of Israel (as often)."[57]

It is worth noting that John 8:24 ("You will die in your sins unless you believe that I am he") seems to echo Is. 43:10-11: "'You are my witnesses,' says the Lord, 'and my servant whom I have chosen, that you may know and believe me and understand that I am He. . . . I, I am the Lord, and besides me there is no savior.'" At the Last Supper Jesus speaks of his coming passion and concludes: "I tell you this now, before it takes place, that when it does take place you may believe that I am he" (John 13:19). As Dodd writes: "It is difficult not to see here an allusion to the divine name ANI-HU. The implication would seem to be that God has given His own Name to Christ; and this is actually stated in 17:11. We may further recall that the Name is associated in the Old Testament with the glory of God."[58]

---

[56] *Supra*, 142.
[57] Dodd, *op. cit.*, 350.
[58] *Ibid.*, 95.

Thus in one of the strongest statements of monotheism, Is. 42:8, we have the statement: "I am the Lord, that is my name; my glory I give to no other, nor my praise to graven images." Now in John 12:23 we have the statement: "The hour has come for the Son of man to be glorified," and this is followed by the prayer: "Father, glorify thy name" (12:28). Later in 17:5 Christ prays: "Father, glorify thou me in thy own presence with the glory which I had with thee before the world was made." It seems quite clear that Jesus is here alluding to the divine name I AM (EGO EIMI=ANI-HU). The presupposition would seem to be that the eternal glory of God is given to Christ, and in the same act the Name of God is glorified.

But we have further to observe the sequel in each case where the name is so used. The EGO EIMI carries with it the solidarity of Christ with God. Thus in John 8:28 we read: "When you have lifted up the Son of Man, then you will know that I am he, and that I do nothing on my own authority but speak thus as the Father taught me." And the next verse reads: "And he who sent me is with me" (cf. Ps. 91:15, "I will be with him in trouble"). In John EGO EIMI seems usually to be followed by an expression of Jesus' solidarity with his Father. Thus in John 13:20, after pronouncing the EGO EIMI, Jesus goes on: "He who receives any one whom I send receives me; and he who receives me receives him who sent me." Other examples are: 16:32, "The hour is coming, and indeed it has come, when you will be scattered, every man to his home, and will leave me alone; yet I am not alone, for the Father is with me"; also 8:16, "Yet even if I do judge, my judgment is true, for it is not I alone that judge but I and he who sent me."

The phrase "I and he who sent me" is equivalent to ANI-WᵉHU as understood in the later tradition. John could have been acquainted with it and this seems to have been the case. The substitution of Jesus for Israel in the expression of solidarity is in harmony with early Christian procedure in general, and in particular with that of the Fourth Gospel. There was a tradition among the Rabbis that while in this age the true name of God is unknown, in the age to come it will be revealed. In the course of his farewell discourse, Jesus lifted his eyes to heaven and declared: "I have manifested thy name to men . . . I make known to them thy name" (17:6, 26). It is difficult not to suppose that there is some reference here to the revelation of the *shem hammephorash*. And the name takes the form, not merely of ANI-HU, EGO EIMI, but of ANI-WᵉHU, "I and he who sent me," since if the name of God is the symbol of his true nature, then the revelation of the name which Jesus gives is that unity of Father and Son to which he bears witness.

"Much of this will seem somewhat speculative," Dodd concludes, "and the links in the chain of evidence are not all complete, but it is at least possible that one of the most distinctive ideas of the Fourth Gospel, and one which has been thought most remote from the Judaism within which Christianity arose, has its roots in reflections of Jewish Rabbis upon prophetic teaching about the relation between God and His people, in the light of the disasters which fell upon Israel during the period A.D. 70–135."[59]

EXALTATION THROUGH SUFFERING

The Brazen Serpent passage (John 3:14-15) is one of the most obvious Exodus passages in the Fourth Gospel. Among a wealth of ideas and associations the passage sets forth the interlocking ideas of being lifted up on the Cross and being lifted up to glory. In some Johannine passages this latter idea is combined with the messianic revelation of the sacred name.

Like the Suffering Servant, Jesus is exalted and glorified in consequence of his passion and death. The association of "lift up" or "exalt" and "glorify" seems to go back to the Greek text of Is. 53. And in primitive Christian usage, Jesus' resurrection and ascension came to be looked upon as phases of his exaltation and glorification. At the Feast of Tabernacles, Jesus declares: "When you have lifted up the Son of Man, then you will know that I AM HE (ANI-HU)" (8:28). One cannot help but bring this into conjunction with Jesus' declaration to Nicodemus: "No one has ascended into heaven but he who descended from heaven, the Son of man. And as Moses lifted up the serpent in the wilderness, so must the Son of man be lifted up" (John 3:14-15). Both contexts speak of the contrast between the "above" and the "below," and of Jesus' departure for the above.

[59] *Ibid.*, 96.

By implication, his journey is a "going up" from the below to above, and hence an exaltation.

In chapter 8, when Jesus announces that he is going whither his hearers cannot come, they surmise that he is contemplating suicide. Aware that his hearers are ready to kill him, Jesus declares: "When you have lifted up the Son of man, then you will know I AM HE" (v. 28). In view of all this, the phrase "when you have lifted up the Son of man" seems to be a grim suggestion that they will help him in his upward way — by killing him. But the manner of his death will be such that then will be manifested the true significance of the mysterious name I AM, understood as the *shem hammephorash*, Ani-w^{e}hu, I and He who sent Me. "That all this would be supposed immediately intelligible to the interlocutors in the dramatic dialogue is unlikely," Dodd admits, "but it is perhaps not too extreme an example of the Johannine irony."[60]

Indeed, it can be argued that the transition from the idea of exaltation to execution and death was a popular play on words. "To lift up someone's head," for example, can be applied to both. In Genesis 40 we see Joseph using the phrase in his interpretation of dreams. In the butler's case it turns out to mean restoration to his butlership, while in the case of the baker it means hanging.

John seems to have used the doctrine of the Name also in his twelfth chapter. This chapter relates the incidents immediately preceding the passion (the anointing at Bethany and the triumphal entry). This sets the stage for the discourse which deals with the single theme of the approaching passion and its significance: the seed that decays to give birth to a crop, the principle of dying to live, exaltation through suffering.

The discourse begins with the statement that among those who went up for the Feast of Passover were some Greeks who expressed a desire to see Jesus. When Jesus hears of this he declares: "The hour has come for the Son of man to be glorified" (John 12:23), and he continues to speak of his death and resurrection.

It is in conquering death by laying down his life that Christ both glorifies God and receives the true glory which comes from God. This glory has no taint of self-glory; rather, it is bound up

---

[60] *Ibid.*, 377.

with the manifestation of the glory of God. An act of self-devotion, this glorification is the judgment of the world. The expulsion of the adversary is fixed. But the final effect of Jesus' exaltation is to draw all mankind to himself. To Nicodemus Jesus had declared: "As Moses lifted up the serpent in the wilderness, so must the Son of man be lifted up" (John 3:14).

So now at the last Passover feast Jesus tells his listeners: "I, when I am lifted up from the earth, will draw all men to myself" (John 12:32). Jesus' listeners rightly understand him to be speaking of death. Again Jesus predicts that many of his hearers will not believe in him. On the other hand, Jesus declares: "He who believes in me, believes not in me but in him who sent me. And he who sees me sees him who sent me" (John 12:44-45).

The Exodus theme is therefore one of the important keys to the understanding of the Fourth Gospel. Indeed, it is St. John who gives the most completely developed typology of the Exodus: "It is to be found on almost every page of his gospel."[61] Jesus stands forth as the New Moses who leads the New Exodus. The prophet like Moses, he gives a New Law far superior to that given by Moses. He gives bread from heaven to the hungry multitudes in the wilderness just as Moses gave manna to the Hebrews. The Light of the World, Jesus goes before the New People of God just as the pillar of fire had gone before their fathers in the wilderness.

Jesus' purpose was to lead the people to the Father. At the beginning of his passion account John writes: "Now before the feast of the Passover, when Jesus knew that his hour had come to depart out of this world to the Father, having loved his own who were in the world, he loved them to the end" (13:1). It would seem that John's phrase "to depart out" receives light from Philo's conception of the Passover as a "passing over."[62]

We are invited to hold in conjunction the Lord's passing through Egypt at the original Passover, the children of Israel's passing out of Egyptian servitude, and Jesus' passing from this world to the Father at the Passover feast. "John makes his own an etymology of the word pasch that Philo had used. To the Jewish philosopher the pasch was the passage, the passage of the Red Sea, the passage from Egypt into the Promised Land.

[61] Cf. Boismard, *supra*, 112.
[62] Cf. Glasson, *op. cit.*, 97f.

Christ's passover was His passage from this world to the Father, from the world of darkness, suffering and death to the Kingdom of Life and Light. When He was 'lifted up' on the Cross, He took the first step that was 'to lift Him' in glory to the right hand of the Father. He passed from earth to heaven not alone but as the head of a new people, as the first of a great multitude. Like a new Moses, Jesus liberated His own. He freed them from this world which is subject to the powers of evil and death so that they can live in the light of God."[63]

[63] M. E. Boismard in Giblet, *op. cit.*, 225.

Epilogue

Searching the Scriptures is truly a discipline. It is not at all a question of setting forth a "new theology," but of discovering *what is there* in the fullest and most meaningful way possible. The Scriptures are something objective, an ever-living norm by which we can test and measure our theologizing, which will always be necessary. Any trend which runs counter to the main lines of Biblical thought should cause the Christian who is thoroughly imbued with Biblical thought to sit up and take notice. It is precisely because we are experiencing a furious drive for a thoroughly secularized, desupernaturalized Christianity, that the Exodus=Wilderness theology is more necessary than perhaps ever before. Paradoxically, it is the Wilderness theology which must determine the proper relationship between the secular city and the Kingdom of God.

An examination of the documents of Vatican II shows that the Wilderness theology was used repeatedly. "Avoiding rigid definitions and scholastic or juridical subtleties, the Council shows a marked preference for vivid and biblical language."[1] In accordance with this general aim, the *Dogmatic Constitution on the Church* sets forth the Church's nature in terms of mystery and people of God. The Church is the new people of God, a concept that is inseparable from the Exodus tradition. And time and time again it is emphasized, echoing a prominent New Testament usage, that the Church is the *pilgrim* people of God. The words "pilgrim" and "pilgrimage" appear a striking number of times.

Every controversialist, of course, has his favorite set of quotes from the documents of Vatican II. In his response to that same *Constitution on the Church*, the noted Methodist observer Dr. Albert C. Outler says that there is the danger that even so mag-

---

[1] Avery Dulles, S.J., Introduction to the Dogmatic Constitution on the Church (*Lumen Gentium*); in, *Documents of Vatican II*, 11.

nificent a document may pass into obscurity, and "there is the equally tragic danger that it may be interpreted and implemented *piecemeal*: that the progressives will stress only its progressive ideas, even as the immobilists attend only to its traditional residues" (*op. cit.* 106). Usually we end up stressing the aspect which we feel is in danger of being lost sight of.

Defining the Church as the new People of God, the *Constitution on the Church* underlines the fact that even this new People of God, living in the last age of the world, is still on pilgrimage, still on the march through the wilderness toward its final goal. "Israel according to the flesh, which wandered as an exile in the desert, was already called the Church of God (2 Esd. 13:1; cf. Num. 20:4; Deut. 23:1ff). Likewise the new Israel which, while going forward in this present world, goes in search of a future and abiding city (cf. Heb. 13:14) is also called the Church of Christ" (cf. Matthew 17:8, § 9). The Church is "now sojourning on earth as an exile" (§ 14). In its chapter on Religious, the document declares: "The People of God has no lasting city here below, but looks forward to one which is to come. This being so, the religious state by giving its members greater freedom from earthly cares more adequately manifests to all believers the presence of heavenly goods already possessed here below" (§ 44).

Chapter VII of the *Constitution on the Church* is entitled: "The Eschatological Nature of the Pilgrim Church and Her Union with the Heavenly Church," and sets forth a system of inaugurated eschatology. "The promised restoration which we are awaiting has already begun in Christ, is carried forward in the mission of the Holy Spirit, and through Him continues in the Church. . . . However, until there is a new heaven and a new earth where justice dwells (cf. 2 Pet. 3:13), the pilgrim Church in her sacraments and institutions, which pertain to this present time, takes on the appearance of this passing world. She herself dwells among creatures who groan and travail in pain until now and await the revelation of the sons of God" (cf. Rom. 8:19-22, § 48). The Virgin Mary is a sign of sure hope and of solace for God's People in pilgrimage" (§ 68).

Always, there remains the question: how is the Christian to deal with the tension between the now and the not yet which is the essential characteristic of the interim age of the Church.

And when you come right down to it, there is no solving all the problems ahead of time. New situations arise, and the Christian is not given the assurance that the search for the will of God will always be smooth and easy. It was inevitable that the Council documents could do little beyond affirming the conviction that the two opposites can and must be held in tension.

This affirmation is made especially in the *Pastoral Constitution on the Church in the Modern World*. The Church teaches that "a hope related to the end of time does not diminish the importance of intervening duties, but rather undergirds the acquittal of them with fresh incentives" (§ 21). "Christ's Church, trusting in the design of the Creator, acknowledges that human progress can serve man's true happiness. Yet she cannot help echoing the Apostle's warning: 'Be not conformed to this world'" (Rom. 12:2). By the word "world" is here meant "that spirit of vanity and malice which transforms into an instrument of sin those human energies intended for the service of God and man" (§ 37). "This Council exhorts Christians, as citizens of two cities, to strive to discharge their earthly duties conscientiously and in response to the gospel spirit. They are mistaken who, knowing that we have here no abiding city but seek one which is to come, think that they may therefore shirk their earthly responsibilities. For they are forgetting that by the faith itself they are more than ever obliged to measure up to these duties, each according to his proper vocation" (§ 43).

In his introduction to the *Decree on Priestly Formation*, Bishop Alexander Carter says that in this document "a real effort is made to do away with any supposed dichotomy between the doctrine of the Church and her practical involvement in time and space and action" (p. 425).

In general it can safely be said that the documents of Vatican II go as far as they possibly can in giving the world its due. Indeed, it is interesting to note that in several instances the responses of Protestant observers include statements that, in their opinion, the documents at times go too far in this direction. In his response to the *Decree on Priestly Formation*, the Lutheran observer Warren A. Quanbeck observes that "one may wonder whether either the declaration on non-Christian religions or the paragraph relating to it in this Decree faces up adequately to the dangers of syncretism" (p. 459). Commenting on the *Decree on the Apostolate of Laity,* Dr. Cynthia Wedel says that she found the paragraphs on the family and on young people less relevant to the realities of today's world than other parts of the document. "I found myself saying 'Yes, but how?' to many of the statements there. It is not the fault of this document alone, however. None of us in the Churches have as yet discovered what to say in these areas of our common life" (p. 524).

But perhaps the most telling criticism was made by Robert McAfee Brown in his response to the *Pastoral Constitution on the Church in the Modern World.* He writes: "Although proper in the context in which it is cited, the statement that 'the Church knows that her message is in harmony with the most secret desires of the human heart' (art. 21), illustrates a temptation throughout the document to assume that the gospel crowns the life of natural man, rather than being, as well, a challenge to, and judgment upon, that life. The document minimizes the degree to which the gospel is also a scandal and a stumbling-block, by which men can be offended as well as uplifted. (At a number of the press conferences in Rome, one could detect a desire on the part of defenders of the *schema* to explain controversial portions in such a way that they would not seem 'offensive.') The making of common cause with others must not be achieved at the price of blunting the uniqueness and distinctiveness of the Christian message.

"In subsequent Catholic reflection upon this problem, then, it can be hoped that the brief references to the relationship of eschatology and ethics (cf. art. 39) will be further developed. Similarly, although the final version is more realistic about man's sin than were earlier drafts, there needs to be more recognition of the pervasiveness of sin in men and human institutions, so that the hopes raised by the tone of the document will not be unnecessarily dimmed by the hard realities of the world. The ongoing power of evil is a theme to which more attention could have been given. If this be Protestant pessimism, it is at least a pessimism we have learned from Scripture and tradition as well as from the daily newspaper" (p. 315f).